THE YOUNG CHILD AS PERSON

The Young Child as Person
Toward the Development of Healthy Conscience

Martha Snyder, M.A.
Ross Snyder, D.D.
Ross Snyder, Jr., B.D., M.D.

 *HUMAN SCIENCES PRESS*
72 Fifth Avenue   3 Henrietta Street
NEW YORK, NY 10011 ● LONDON, WC2E 8LU

Printed in the United States of America
0123456789   987654321

Library of Congress Cataloging in Publication Data

Snyder, Martha.
  The young child as person: toward the development of healthy conscience

  Bibliography: p. 229
  Includes index.
  1. Moral development. 2. Conscience.
3. Self-actualization (Psychology) 4. Child
psychology. 5. Child psychopathology. 6. Education,
Preschool. I. Snyder, Ross, joint author.
II. Snyder, Ross, 1931– joint author. III. Title.
[DNLM: 1. Child psychology. 2. Child development.
WS105.3 S675p]
BF723.M54S63   155.4'18   LC 79-15779
ISBN 0-87705-466-5

To Our Children
And Our Children's Children

CONTENTS

Preface

This book is written for those who want to help children function with vitality that comes from inner feelings and meanings, and to care deeply for others. It provides insights and enabling processes for helping the child realize self-as-person. Methods for releasing children who are withdrawn and for healing the hostile acting child are included. These theories and methods come out of nursery school living. They apply equally well in the home.

This book is about real children. Some are black, some white, some Oriental. Many of the children are happy and well-adjusted, some suffer from emotional injuries that have caused them to withdraw so that they will not be hurt further. Others are full of hostility turning to bitterness and want to hurt back the world that has hurt them. Others live as if the mist of creation has not cleared and individuation has not yet taken place.

In every child is a thrust to actualize his or her potential, and live in relationship. This potential can flow free and nourish creative living, or it can become disturbed, choked, and person destroying. In our relationship with children we are saying in effect to each child, "You are meant to be expressive spontaneity carrying out your life projects by way of creating with others, and you are meant to like the taste of yourself while doing so."

Our method of being with children is grounded in our understanding of personhood, healthy conscience, and how a justice culture enables these. Each chapter of the book contains a fundamental part of this theory, along with the actual dialogue that took place in the school. The reader can be present in the living experience and see the theory functioning. It is important that the reader concentrate on the idea structure of this book, as well as pay attention to the immediate method of being with children presented in the many illustrative incidents.

Many of our insights and enabling processes are grounded in existential phenomenology. The existentialist is concerned that a child realize his or herself as a personal center. Phenomenology helps us understand how important it is to help children transform experiences into meanings and learn how to do it on their own.

An important concept that organizes our style of nurturing children is the concept of Life World. Each child has the task of putting together a meaningful world which he or she then tries to live. Once teachers understand that a child is always living a particular Life World at any given moment, busy organizing the next possible Life World, they have power to live differently with children.

A basic method in helping a child grow is understanding the personal existence of the child. Understanding affirms the child and prevents him from feeling rejected or alone. He feels a part of the main stream of life in the school in which all are learning to play and have fun together. Understanding develops feelings and processes them into meanings out of which the child lives. With increased power of understanding, children become agents of their own becoming. They begin to take account of the inner world of others. They are equipped to take part in establishing a culture.

We use many of Carl Roger's insights into the process of understanding. Understanding is a much more multileveled process than we once thought. We have developed two levels of understanding that are very useful in working with children —understanding the child's existence situation, and reconstructing the episode with feelings included.

One chapter of the book is devoted to the growth of conscience. In a world that today appears so devoid of conscience by which life together can be mutually ordered, with too many people living out of anger, dominated by a biting, accusing conscience that is continually cramping and destroying them and others, healthy conscience becomes a major concern of human development. Erikson pointed out that the years from three to five are of special importance in the formation of conscience. A child's growing must go beyond just the developmental task of individual initiative.

We believe conscience formation to be a central task of the nursery school. Significant aspects of the process of conscience formation include the experience of appreciative caring, the understanding mode of conversation, participation in the formation of a justice culture, and integrity or "truth work," as well as encountering a personal presence and becoming aware of the highest and the best.

The nursery school as a justice culture is the ground out of which conscience develops. George Herbert Mead pointed out in his social theory of personal growth that we become "person" and create society through common understandings of experiences, persons, and enterprises. These become "significant symbols," part of a common usable vocabulary with which we feel and think and solve our problems. With them we can organize a world to be lived. The children within the nursery school do not use the words "justice culture." But as a result of shared experiences and working out problems together within the moral structure of the nursery school, "justice culture" becomes a lived symbol.

Our understanding of conscience incorporates Heidegger's concept of conscience as the "call of possibility" and the Freudian view of conscience as the interiorization of the valuings of significant adults. It builds on John Dewey's understanding that values are taught by the way schools are organized and governed.

We also understand conscience is based on the person's understanding of self and others. It is the meaning of the self-in-world that determines how a person interprets events and acts. Therefore increasing self-esteem and competence, increasing the understanding and appreciation of others, developing an accurate picture of the world, and learning valuable skills in communication and problem solving, facilitate healthy conscience.

The development of conscience therefore is more than clarifying values, interiorizing parental do's and don'ts, memorizing platitudes, doing verbal exercises in moral reasoning, having problem behavior corrected, or rewarding acceptable behavior. When we read descriptions of stages of cognitive and moral reasoning, it is important that we do not conclude that conscience development is a step-wise linear process, or that young children are not capable of truly moral behavior since they lack the highest cognitive or abstract reasoning skills. Young children do spontaneously care about others. They also act according to ethical principles even though they cannot articulate them.

Much of the advice given today about the care, discipline, and moral development of young children lacks a basic understanding of what a person is, what type and content of conscience is to be encouraged, and what functions culture performs. As a result, the methods recommended are often partial and ultimately misleading—failing to bring about personalization as well as socialization, rich sociality as well as interiority, receptivity *and* functional autonomy, deep caring *and* power to form worlds.

What is learned foremost is a quality of spirited aliveness. A child learns personal existence as an interactive whole.

The existential phenomenology of William James makes clear some foundations of such fullness. In harmony with his thought, a school good for young children would be rich in the following kinds of activities: "Direct relationship" with life pulsing. Children, at their own pace, enterprising live options that stretch their powers. Being "up to something", and inviting others to join in. Understanding, talking over, conceptualizing their experiencings as they happen. Recovering from dark moments and resisting being profaned. In touch with something solid and trustworthy within the self. Beginnings of essential capacity to believe in people. Such children are not thrown by problem situations, rather social radiance and poise become their life-style.

In a democracy, every child is to become capable of self-propelling moral living. How this can happen is being freshly opened up as a mainline conversation in American society. The resources to work out common views with other people right in situation, to appreciate the integrity of another, to live out of meanings instead of egotism or commands, to invent enterprises and worlds-to-live that leap with imagination, to build toward a culture and a conscience that will enable children to come through the tough times ahead—not merely as surviving but as generative—all these are what this book is about.

It is written for people in the field of education who deal with the developmental story of life, and for those who train teachers of young children. The book is for use by teaching staffs of nursery schools and day care centers as throughout the year they work on the ideas and strategies from which their programs develop. It is also for parents. It could be the agenda for a group of parents who would like to achieve a viewpoint and method of living with children that make parenting a profession of faith, a satisfaction, and one meaning of life.

Rather than interrupt the flow of the book with isolated footnotes explaining terminology and its derivation, we have placed a synopsis of six basic concepts at the end of the book. This synopsis defines the important components of each basic concept so that it can be understood in its totality. It will be helpful to those who are working on applying the book's basic theory and explaining it to others.

This book is a documented report of faith in children and a certain way of living with their growing. Here are views, deep down understandings, ways of building a world with children that make of them something other than nerve-racking problems and hindrances to adult fulfullment.

Children are a magnificence beyond our capacity to imagine, but not beyond our capacity to participate in their growth. Each is a bundle of potential that wants very much to succeed and be part of humanity. They want to be in on the fun. Each morning they arrive with vitality bringing all their hopes and doubts. A nursery school teacher, a parent, is priviliged to be entrusted with so much yearning potential.

Part I

TOWARD SPIRITED EXISTENCE

TOWARD SPIRITUAL EXISTENCE

Chapter 1

ESSENTIAL CONVICTIONS ABOUT CHILDREN

Every child wants to function.

Every child wants to be in relationship.

There is an exciting world to explore.

These three convictions are basic for working with children. With some help and a warm environment, healthy growth will happen. Again and again in a good nursery school, there are these kind of events.

> One morning four-year-old Danny, wearing a fireman's hat, walks up to four-year-old Sam as he arrives. Danny's face is alive with expectation.
>   Danny: "Do you want to play Rescue Boys?"
> Their smiles meet. Spontaneously they shake hands with much energy. Sam gets a fireman's hat and they jump on the green box for a helicopter and are off rescuing imaginary people in distress. Other children join the play. After each important feat they shake hands again.

Potential is meeting potential. Each is being enriched by contact with another potential. It is a group of equals doing important things together. The world is filled with possibilities.

EVERY CHILD WANTS TO FUNCTION

In every child is a thrust to actualize his or her potential. Potential is always there and is hungry for expression. When a child sees other children having fun, he or she wants the fun also.

> Susan watches the boys playing Superman and Batman at the active end of the room. They are jumping off the green box. Two of them hold onto the ends of a short rope and jump together. This looks like fun to Susan. She works hard to climb up on the box.
>
> | Sam: | "You can't be Superman. You are a girl." |
> |---|---|
> | Susan: | "I'm Supergirl." |
>
> Sam accepts this. When the boys jump she doesn't have the nerve. It looks too high. I speak softly to her.
>
> | Mrs. S: | "Susan, if you turn on your stomach, you can slide down." |
> |---|---|
> | | (She does.) |
> | Susan: | "I came down this way, Mrs. Snyder." |
> | Mrs. S: | "Yes, now you know how to get up and how to get down." |
>
> The boys are so busy with their play, they do not notice how Susan got up and down. In a short time she too is jumping off the box. It is an important morning for Susan. She learns she can risk doing daring things. It is also fun to play with strong boys.

The potential was abundantly present in Susan. All she needed was the stimulation of something exciting going on to awaken it. She also needed a little help to start her on the way of succeeding.

In some children results of past experiences hold back a child from using his potential.

Carl is an attractive, physically well-built boy. He talks a great deal about being strong and goes around wearing a Batman cape and showing the children his muscle. If play gets rough he goes to the quieter end of the room. John likes Carl and would like to play with him, so John comes up to Carl and starts to wrestle in a friendly way. Carl backs away.

Mrs. S:	"John, you want to play and have fun with Carl. You don't want to hurt him. Carl, if you just push John back, like this, that is the way to wrestle so it is fun."
Carl:	"See my muscle."
	(Talking to me, not to John, he bends his arm and flexes his muscle.)
Mrs. S:	"If it gets too rough, you can always say 'Stop, I don't want to play anymore,' and you would stop, wouldn't you John?"
John:	"Yes."

But Carl walks away showing his muscle to the girls, telling them how strong he is.

Carl wants very much to be strong. He is trying to talk himself into believing it, but he is afraid. The potential and desire are there. Somehow he has gotten the message into his feeling structure that if he tries and fails it will be disastrous. He is afraid of getting hurt even though he is as strong as John. He would rather not try than fail. He is unaware of the potential inside him. He needs success experiences to build a feeling of competency before he will be ready to wrestle with John in fun.

In some children potential is beautifully available for use.

In the autumn quarter, Becky, the youngest girl in the school, watches the boys climbing the tree in the school yard. John is a good climber and goes up high. Melvin tries to follow him. He climbs to the top of the aluminum ladder but is afraid to step up into the tree. He turns and starts down.

> Mrs. S: "Some day, you will figure out how to do it,
>   Melvin?"

Becky watches carefully. She goes up the ladder and up into the tree. She seems so fragile to be climbing a tree, but she is doing it with a great deal of self-assurance. Her dark eyes flash with excitement and satisfaction.

Even when a child is trying to actualize his potential, sometimes exterior forces keep working against him.

At the beginning of the morning John arrives with Bella, one of the ladies who takes care of him. She brings him inside the school and says that John had messed his pants yesterday at home. I could see that it is difficult for John to listen to her tell me this. He hangs his head. (At the beginning of the school year, I tell parents I am always glad to talk with them about their child, but not when the child is present.)

> Mrs. S: (When Bella leaves) "You don't like to have
>   Bella tell me those kind of things about you, do
>   you, John?" John doesn't answer.
> Mrs. S: "Most of the time you have your bowel move-
>   ments in the toilet. That was an accident, wasn't
>   it?"
> John: (In a strong voice) "Yes."

John had never messed his pants in school. Knowing him, I could be sure it was an accident.
Later in the morning while playing in the sink, John is still working on this. He is playing with a little red diver.

> John: "Mrs. Weaver, there is a rotor man. He is very
>   strong. Nobody can hurt him."
>   (As if this is what he wanted to be.)
> Mrs. W: "You really are quite strong, John."
> John: "Yes."

He does not want to get hurt by Bella. He kept struggling to get rid of the feelings she is forcing upon him.

Without self-esteem, it is difficult for a child to use his potential. Bella had invaded his school world where he feels good about·himself and where he gets a chance to actualize his imagination and powers. We had to help John recover his self-esteem and stand up for himself. Education is concerned with helping a child find a method of meeting life. We were trying to help John become empowered to handle whatever situation he finds himself in.

Every Child Wants to Be in Relationship

Alienation, which is "being out of relationship," is hell. It is a state of existence that affects virtually every aspect of a person's life. Every child wants to "be in relationship," to *be* relationship, not just to survive or cope. When children "are in relationship" they are a kind of existence that is free to be alive with others, with the world of nature, and with the world of ideas. They are free to create and be created. When we speak of relationship in the singular in this book we are referring to this most basic and yearned for human reality.

Children want to be in relationship with the significant adults in their world as well as with their peers. Children are miserable when they feel out of relationship. Then they are apt to resort to old behavior patterns that do not work such as attacking, crying, or withdrawing. Children want adults who will enable them to stay in relationship.

John and Sam are energetic boys. They like each other and want very much to play together. But sometimes the going gets rough. One day Sam is riding around on the "Big Wheel" and John is on a tricycle. They get into trouble. John starts to cry hard. I had never seen him cry so hard before. He is holding his face as Sam rides away.

Mrs. S: "John, Sam did something that hurt you?"
John: (Sobbing very hard) "yes."
        (I give him time to recover.)

Mrs. S:	"You couldn't think of anything you could say to make him stop?"
John:	"No."
Mrs. S:	"You could say, 'Hey, that hurts. Stop it!' " (Sam comes by on the "Big Wheel.")
Mrs. S:	"Sam, John says you hurt him in the face."
Sam:	"He was shooting me with his finger."
Mrs. S:	"John, Sam says you were shooting at him and he doesn't like being shot at. That's why he hit you."
John:	"Yes."

And it is over. John thought that he was playing, but now he understands why Sam hit him. They can play together again.

Getting hit in the face is bad, but not as bad as being out of relationship. It was very meaningful to John to have someone his age to play with. At home, he had to come to terms with older brothers, but in Sam he found a friend he could match his potential with as an equal. Sam made him feel strong and alive. It was a disintegrating experience to have this relationship threatened. It was like destroying his new self.

Terry is a four-year-old with great potential. She is attractive and physically well developed, and she has a beautiful singing voice. But she does not know how to play with her peers. Somewhat frequent absences keep breaking relationships, but in the spring she begins to feel secure and strong. One day she is standing on the jungle gym.

Terry:	"I'm bigger than John. I could beat up on him."
Mrs. W:	"You are feeling strong now, Terry?"
Terry:	"Yes, I'm bigger than all the kids. I could beat up on them all."
Mrs. W:	"You really are strong. But it would be more fun to play with them."
Terry:	(In a longing way) "You know, it really would."

No child enjoys being a wall flower. Potential has a strong urge to grow. But at the same time the child wants to be actualized in relationship to others. Potential allowed to run wild at the expense of relationship to others is destructive to the person. For the child to learn how to actualize his imagination and projects, and at the same time to be in relationship with people, is an achievement that has life-long effects.

THERE IS AN EXCITING WORLD TO EXPLORE

The real world is more exciting than any fairyland. It is full of surprises and obstacles against which children can match their strength. It includes all kinds of people and the world of nature. From contacts with the real, the young child builds a life world from which he or she lives. The real world and a child's potential go together.

Children's play is contagious at school. One child gets an idea and the creativity of others gets going.

Diane is gathering up small sticks in the school yard. She brings them to me.

| Diane: | (Handing me one stick at a time) "This is a shark. This is a porpoise." |
| Mrs. S: | "Those are the biggest fish you could have caught." |

Other children join the play and bring lots of fish.

Diane:	"Now I'm going to get a rattlesnake."
Mrs. S:	"If you get a rattlesnake, you'd better be careful how you pick it up so it doesn't bite you because they are poisonous."
Diane:	"I know how to handle rattlesnakes." (In a short time she comes back with a piece of vine.) "This is a dead rattlesnake."
Mrs. S:	"Then it is safe for me to hold it."

She goes off in search of some more interesting things.

Imagination can soar in the real world and bring a child into relationship. The world becomes exciting to some children through the imaginative play of others. Things are no longer just objects.

Early in the school year Terry asks me to help her build a house with our big blocks. I start to help her, and other children join the play. After the house is built they get dolls and start to play. I stay in the play to help the new children learn to play together. We are washing the dolls and putting on pretend talcum powder.

Terry:	"This isn't a real house, is it?"
Mrs. S:	"No, but we are pretending it is real."
Terry:	"This isn't a real bath tub, is it?"
Mrs. S:	"No, it is a pretend bath tub."
Terry:	"This isn't a real baby, is it?"
Mrs. S:	"The way we are playing with the doll makes it seem real?"
Terry:	"Yes."

She joins the play and starts to wash and dress a doll.

Terry:	"This is a real house. This is the inside of a real house, Mrs. Snyder."

She has caught the spirit and the situation seems very real. She was absorbed in a meaningful world.

The real world is not all good; it includes things that are scary and destructive. In school, children's fears often get expressed in their play and get played out until the tension is gone.

Annabel is a bright blond 4-year-old who could read when she started school. One morning, Annabel is playing in the jungle house inside the school.

Annabel:	(Excited) "There is a robber trying to get me!"

Mrs. S: "What are you going to do about that robber?"
Annabel: "I'm going to knock on the window and make
           him go away."
           (She knocks.)
           "Now he has gone away."
           (A moment later)
           "Now he's dead."
Mrs. S: "You knocked so he would go away. He's dead
           now. Another thing you could always do is to go
           to the telephone and tell the police to come. You
           could tell them that there is a robber outside
           your house and he is trying to get in."
Annabel: "I'll do that."
           (She pretends to call the police.) "Come get the
           robber outside."
           (A few seconds later)
           "They got him!"

In a group of children who care for each other, the potential of all is available to solve problems.

In the spring Carl drops his prized cowboy belt down the ventilator in the yard of the school. The ventilator is a five-foot square cement hole that goes down six feet into the ground and is covered by a strong iron grill. Carl is very upset about losing his belt and he starts to cry hard. The children gather around and look down at the belt at the bottom of the hole. They know from experience that the top is too heavy to open.

Mrs. W: "Oh, Carl, that is your wonderful cowboy belt
           down there. We will have to figure a way to get
           it out."
Billy: "Get a vine, Diane, and we can get it out."

Both of them pull a dead vine from the wall and carefully put it through one of the small holes in the top of the ventilator. But is is not long enough.

Billy: "If we had two vines."

Like a flash they both run for another vine and twist the two together. This time the vine touches the belt but does not pick it up.

> Diane: "We need something on the end."

She takes the big safety pin off her plaid skirt and tries to fasten it to the vine, but it drops and falls into the ventilator also. The children come and get me. With real concern, they show me the belt and the safety pin. But it is time to go home; mothers are beginning to arrive.

> Mrs. S: "Oh my, Carl, your beautiful belt and Diane, your gold safety pin, down there. Maybe when Dr. Snyder comes tomorrow, he can figure out a way to help you get them out."

The next morning as soon as Dr. Snyder walks into school, they take him to see Carl's belt.

> Dr. S: "I think we can figure out a way to get them. Maybe we can find something in the cupboard that will help."
> (They go to the cupboard and he takes out one of our strong round magnets.)
> "You know what magnets do?"
> Carl: "They pick up nails and metal things."
> Dr. S: "Can you think of a way to use the magnet to get the belt?"
> Billy: "We can tie it to a string."
> (He jumps up and down. So does Carl. As others get the idea, they too jump up and down.)
> Dr. S: "We need something stronger than string. Let's try this wire."

He fastens the long wire to the magnet. All the children want to help. Dr. Snyder lets Carl fish out the belt by swinging the magnet onto the buckle. When Carl pulls up the belt and safety pin, he can hardly control his excitement. All the children are excited. Magnets are no longer just playthings for picking up nails; they can also be used for actual work. A group of children with the aid of an adult has joined together to solve a problem.

The real world, like a child's potential, is inexhaustable. The young child welcomes help that will enable him or her

To function

To stay in relationship

To explore the exciting world of people and objects.

Chapter 2

PULSE OF LIFE

The young child is an exploring, observing, interacting, feeling, thinking person. Wherever a three- or four-year-old looks, there is something exciting to see, to try out, and find out what it is for.

The nursery school is a place where the pulse of life is sensed and celebrated. Encountering the wonders of existence, the beauty and mystery of life and birth, the joy of music, and the fun of movement, pulses life-enabling energies. One of the goals of nursery school is to help a child feel life pulsing within, and animating his community and his world.

Even common everyday water possesses this rich wondrous possibility for the young child. Water—that runs over the tops of things, splashes, spills, falls down. You can dam up, throw it up in the air, and catch it in a pan again (or at least part of it). That you step in. That will drip off the table. That a sponge will absorb, and a boat will float in, but not a rock. That you can wear a raincoat in. That splashes on an umbrella, makes bubbles, freezes and then you can slide on. That gets you wet and you can change your clothes. That rains down from the sky and makes puddles. You can drink it out of the faucet, it gushes out of water spouts, you can take a bath in it, you can squirt it out of a bottle, it goes through the sand. When you pour in paint it changes color. It makes things disappear like salt or sugar, you can sprinkle it out of a hose. It makes wonderful mud. . . .

This wonderful world has dogs in it, too. Not just one dog, but millions of dogs and cats, elephants, birds, and cold germs that are so small you can't see them. And worms that don't have eyes or ears or legs, which you can dig up in the dirt and hold in your hand. And polliwogs that turn into frogs that can hop. And worms that turn into butterflies.

> Gretchen: "Not worms, Mrs. Snyder. Caterpillars turn into butterflies."
>
> Mrs. S: "That's right, it is caterpillars that turn into butterflies."

This wonderful world has people in it. People who are fun and good to be with—like daddy, mommy, babies, brothers, sisters, grandmothers, and grandfathers. There are also people who are cross, perhaps because they are sick or need someone to be kind to them. And then there are people who are just mean. It is hard to know why.

MYSTERY OF LIFE

Part of this pulsing world is the mystery of seeds. In our school we cut open a big pumpkin to see what is inside. We take out the seeds. Some of the children are not so sure at first about getting their hands in the goo. But I say, "It is fun to get all gooey sometimes. It washes off." Then we plant some of the seeds and wait for them to grow. On the day we open the pumpkin, we put small pumpkins around the play yard so each child can choose one to take home and show the family what is inside.

We shell corn and plant it. Children enjoy shelling corn, so we do it several times during the year.

One Monday morning, Jay came in and saw how much our corn had grown over the weekend.

Jay: (Holding his arms high) "The corn will grow as
        tall as a tree."

I should have replied, "Isn't it wonderful that seeds grow?" because he had captured the feeling of mystery that I had hoped for. Instead I responded scientifically, "Jay, corn doesn't grow as tall as a tree. It grows about as tall as your dad."

The children enjoy milkweed seeds because they have parachutes and the wind can carry them out of sight. Locust seeds are fun because they come in pods and rattle. When the seeds start to grow, the children take them home in a paper cup. The locust seed is special because it can become a tree. "How can there be a tree in such a small seed?" they wonder.

And there are babies. "Pumpkins grow from pumpkin seeds. Corn grows from corn. Locust trees grow from locust seeds. Babies grow from an egg inside the mother. The mother's egg is very small and the daddy's sperm that joins the egg is even smaller. When the two join the baby starts to grow in the mother's uterus. It is not the stomach. The baby's head is down and the seat is up. When the baby is old enough to be born, the baby comes out the vagina between the legs of the mother. The doctor helps it get born. He cuts off the umbilical cord and puts on a bandage. When the cut heals it becomes the navel or belly button. Everyone has one. If the baby has a penis and testicles, it is a boy. If it has a vagina, there is a uterus inside and it is a girl. They dress the baby and put it in a crib. The mother and father give the baby a name. That is how babies grow. Isn't it a wonderful world!" We have put this story into a book with pictures, called *How Things Grow,* which we use in the nursery school.

Pulse of life includes a child's feelings about sex. Giving the child the right words to use about his bodily functions is part of this attitude of respect. Good toilet terms are an important part of sex education. Before the year starts, I write a letter to the parents with information about the school. I tell them that the toilet terms we use at school are go to the toilet, urinate, wet, penis, rectum, vagina, and BM or bowel movement.

BODIES

I have discovered that the children get interested in anything I enjoy and am interested in. They can understand anything that I know enough about to explain to them. One spring day, Jessie brought me a stick she had found in the yard. I was busy and didn't pay much attention to it until she offered it to me and said, "Smell it, Mrs. Snyder." Then I noticed it was a live branch. I showed her the green part under the bark and told her that a tree does not have blood; it has sap. The sap is the food for the tree and it travels up under the bark to the tall branches at the very top of the tree. I pointed to the top of our tree.

The following Monday, Jessie's mother asked me if we had been talking about blood at school.

"I don't think so," I said.

"Oh yes you were. Saturday Jessie grabbed me around the legs and said, 'Mommie, your big fat seat has blood in it, but a tree doesn't have blood, it has sap.'"

This episode made me think that the children might like to see what a person looks like on the inside. We had a medical booklet at home that used cellophane overlays to show the inside of a person. I was not sure that this would be scary to children, so I decided to show it to Jessie first. She usually arrived early. When she saw the book on the table, she wanted to know what it was.

"This is not a story book, Jessie. This shows pictures of what a person looks like on the inside. See, this is what a person looks like under the skin." I pointed to the lungs. "These are the lungs. The air comes in the nose and goes down into the lungs when you breathe." I showed her where my lungs were and how when I breathed, they go up and down. She showed me hers. "And these are the intestines. The food goes down the throat, into the stomach here, and then into the intestines, and what is left over comes out as a bowel movement. This is the heart. It pumps blood through the arteries to all parts of the body." I opened and closed my fist as I told her how the heart pumps the blood. I told her that the heart beats all day and all night.

Around this time, another child arrived and wanted to know what we were reading. Jessie said to her, "This is not a story book. This shows you what a person looks like on the inside." She showed her the lungs, intestines, and heart, using almost my exact words and motions.

I realized that the subject was not scary or beyond children of this age. So *Trans-Visions of Anatomical Chromographs*, originally intended for medical students, has become one of the most interesting books of our school. Not all children are ready for it; some three-year-olds will go on playing with cars while we are looking at it. But in the course of the year, most of the children will know something about the inside of a person. Later when the children play doctor they use a real stethoscope to check up on the heart and lungs.

From these experiences, the children became interested in the inside of other things—our record player, a clock, even one of our dead frogs.

We try to keep learning as experiential as possible, believing that first-hand contact with the real in its natural environment is much better than sitting a child down at a table to stimulate his sensory perceptions. It is through distinct experiences that the child develops concepts and meanings.

> In the springtime the children noticed buds on our trees. I pulled down a branch so that they could see and touch them.
>
> "These are buds. See, they have very little leaves on the inside. They will grow and the tree will be full of leaves. Leaves are the tree's lungs. They absorb oxygen and carbon dioxide from the air."
>
> Later I heard Van talking to a boy in the neighborhood. They were playing with a wagon in his back yard when the boy started to pull leaves from the tree.

> Van: "You don't pull leaves off of trees. Those are the tree's lungs."
>
> Boy: "We need them to put in the wagon."
>
> Van: "We can use rocks."

Van had transformed the information that had come to him with delight and respect into a meaning, which he was using in other situations.

In children's play together, they discover each other.

> One day in the bathroom, some of the children were washing their hands.

> Sue: "Evan's skin is black."
>
> Mrs. S: "Yes, and I like it.
> (Evan was pleased to hear me say this. He was radiant and pulled up his shirt to show his tummy.)
>
> Sue: "Even his belly button is black."
>
> Mrs. S: "Yes, and I like it."

> They played together and the good feelings continued. Black skin became something which is part of another self.

In the springtime the children discovered worms in our school yard. They enjoyed digging in the ground to find them.

Estelle put hers in a paper cup to put in her lawn at home. The next day, we had the following conversation:

Estelle:	(Very disappointed) "Mrs. Snyder, my mother is afraid of worms. She doesn't like them."
Mrs. S:	"Maybe if you explained to her that worms don't have any eyes, or ears or legs, she would think that they were interesting."
Estelle:	(Seeming very anxious to have her mother appreciate them) "I'll tell her."
Mrs. S:	"Worms are also good for the lawn because they loosen the soil when they dig, and air gets to the roots of the grass."
Estelle:	"I'll tell her."

To Estelle, worms were part of a wonderful world and she wanted her mother to enjoy and respect them too.

Children use these encounters with reality to develop concepts and meanings. They do not come from abstract naming or controlled "learning." A child needs to be part of a meaningful world. Meanings come not from geometrical space but from lived space.

DEATH

Death often makes its appearance early in the life of a child: "What happened to Grampa? Won't I be able to sit on his lap?" A child needs an explanation of death so that the world does not become an unpredictable, fearsome place. Parents need to make some kind of interpretation at this time according to their own beliefs. It can be damaging if the mood of a home changes without explanation because the parents think a three-year-old is too young to talk about death. Since I do believe in a life after death in some form, I explain it this way when the occasion arises.

Mrs. Carry brings Polly and Ned to school. Mrs. Carry says Ned's mother wants me to know that Ned would not be in school tomorrow because Ned's grandfather has died and his family is going to Michigan. I try to say something to Ned about death, but he didn't seem to be listening, so I stop. Outside, near the end of the morning, I sit down on the air vent to scrape mud off the children's shoes.

Dick: "Where is Ned going to go tomorrow?"

Polly: "Why do people die?"

Mrs. S: "Ned's grandfather was old and his body wore out. The doctors did everything they could to make him better. But his body was so worn out that he died. When the body dies, the real part goes on to be with God."

Polly: "Will I get a new body?"

Mrs. S: "Nobody knows for sure, Polly. All we know is that the real part goes on."

Jill: "Tell it all over again about Ned going to see his grandfather."

So I did. Ned now seemed to sense what had happened.

Ned: "Will my father die?"

Mrs. S: "Your father is still young. Only old people whose bodies are worn out die. Or sometimes people who get badly hurt in an accident die."

Jill: "Is my father young?"

Mrs. S: "Yes, your father is still young and he probably won't die until you grow up and get married and have children of your own. Then your father will be their grandfather."

Polly: "Say it all over again, Mrs. Snyder."

And so I go over it again.

Some parents who do not believe in life after death explain death this way. After talking about Grandpa's illness and death, they go on to say, "Life is a wonderful thing. Everything that lives finally dies. We don't know why, but that is the way it is. We would have liked to have Grandpa live longer. We will remember him and always love him."

Death is strange to a child. His energies have been centered on learning to live, then suddenly he is faced with death as part of life. This is a serious matter to him and he needs help to deal with it. The feeling tones of the adult to whom the child is talking are important because he is apt to incorporate them.

The child's major question is, "Will I or my parents die soon?" This question needs to be answered. It is helpful to give the child a time perspective on the possible story of his life. Children like to know that they probably will live to be a mother or daddy and even become a grandmother or a grandfather.

Talking over some of the happy experiences the child had with the person who died will help keep alive the real relationship. This relationship should never be ruined in the future by using it to control a child's behavior by saying things such as, "Grandpa would not like to see you acting this way."

If a child's questions are answered simply but honestly, death will not become morbid but something that is part of life. I try hard never to use the words "sleep" or "bed" in my explanation of death because some children may associate death with going to bed or to sleep.

One day, Jill is playing cowboy.

> Jill: "Cowboys don't die, they just keep on shooting."
> Mrs. S: "Cowboys on TV don't seem to die, Jill. But real
>   cowboys do, if they get shot and the doctor can't
>   fix them like if they get shot in the heart."

MONSTERS: SEPARATING THE UNREAL FROM THE REAL

There is another form of deathing done to children. Their pulse of life becomes tense from violence programed on television. They are taught to expect that brutality is the way they will be treated by the world. Just as they are beginning to feel good about themselves and secure in the world, along comes another monster contrived by the money-making world that upsets or destroys their basic trust that the world is not hostile. The child is still working on basic trust and should not have it destroyed just as it is beginning to form. Just when the child most needs a mother and father, many parents are rushing off to "fulfill themselves." The child needs relaxed conversation and fun, rather than being left with destructive fears about reality.

At juice time we sit down at the table as a group for juice and crackers. This conversation took place.

Jim:	"Mrs. Snyder, King Kong is scary."
Tess:	(Demonstrating in a dramatic way) "He has sharp teeth and long fingernails."
Mrs. S:	"They really make him look as ugly as they can by making him have teeth sticking out and long claws?"
Steve:	"He gets in my closet at night and I'm afraid."
Tess:	"I scream, then my daddy comes and gets in bed with me."
Dan:	"We have two television sets. My daddy has a little one. We watch it on the little one. When King Kong gets in my closet I just say 'come out and we will be friends.' "
Jim:	"King Kong gets in my bed so I sleep under the bed. Then my dad whips me."
Mrs. S:	"He is so scary you want to get away from him. Even though he is only pretend, they make him seem so real he does seem real."

It took three days in a row to help them handle King Kong. They would say he was only pretend and just a costume. But it took a lot of thinking through on their part to relieve their fear. Then I made up a song to the tune of Old McDonald that they sang with vigor and appropriate motions.

Old King Kong is an old scary guy
Eee-i-ee-i-o
He has sharp teeth and long fingernails
Eee-i-ee-i-o

With a grrr here and a grrr there
"I'll get you here," and "I'll get you there."
Old King Kong is a mean old beast
(Scream)

Old King Kong is just a big bluff
Eee-i-ee-i-o
You punch him in the stomach
and kick him in the seat
Eee-i-ee-i-o
With a punch-kick here and a
punch-kick there. Here a
punch-kick, there a punch-kick,
everywhere a punch-kick
Old King Kong is just a big bluff
Fooey (Shout)

IDEAS

Part of this wonderful world is also ideas that you can have
and enjoy with others.

Four boys are sitting on top of the jungle house. It is near the
end of the spring quarter and lately they have been starting the
morning this way. They are talking in an intimate way. They
seem like a group of men in deep discussion. Then their tone of
voice becomes more excited and argumentative. Some are saying
"It is," others "It isn't." I feel they are learning to hold their own
by talking. Finally Dick calls to me in desperation.

Dick: "Mrs. Snyder, isn't infinitude a number?"
Mrs. S: "Well, not exactly Dick. Infinity is like—some-
         thing that goes on and on. It's sort of like the sky,
         it goes on and on and there doesn't seem to be
         any end."
Russ: "The clouds are the top of the sky."
Mrs. S: "The clouds seem to be the top of the sky but
         when you go up in an airplane, it goes above the
         clouds."
Myles: "Mine went through the clouds."

Mrs. S: "Even the astronauts that went to the moon couldn't find the end of the sky. It just went on and on."
Dick: "Yep!"
Russ: "Yep!"

The argument is over. They are ready for the next adventure.

CELEBRATING AND MUSIC

Celebrating the good things in life can become a way of life. Much of life can be entered into with fun.

One morning the children arrive full of excitement.

Bess: "It's snowing! And the snow is all over everything!"
Gloria: "I rode my sled!"
Russ: "It came over my boots."
Mrs. S: "Just look at our yard!"
Jay: "It's on our slide!"
Gloria: "It's all over the tree!"
Russ: "Let's go step in it."

So we put on the snowsuits again and go out to enjoy it. Celebration seems right in a climate of appreciation and adventure.

Some growth takes real effort. We celebrate when a child makes some significant growth or does something for the first time. It encourages self-appreciation and respect.

One morning Ben succeeds in putting on his own snowsuit.

Mrs. S: "Ben, you put on your whole snowsuit all by yourself. Even your boots. I didn't have to help you with anything. Wowie!"

One needs to call attention to what the child did rather than how pleased you are or tell him what a big boy he is now. Otherwise, the next time he fails at something he is apt to feel that he is still little and not so good.

> For weeks Grant watched the other boys climb on top of the green box and jump off, but he did not try it. One morning he put two blocks next to the green box, cautiously stepped on them and jumped off. He was pleased with himself. I was pleased because I knew this was his first attempt to go higher. He smiled. I smiled back.
>
>   Student Teacher: "You did jump, Grant!"

Appreciating and celebrating accomplishments is appropriate and enhances a healthy sense of competence. Praising compliance or obedience runs the risk of producing an other-directed, praise-seeking child.

Birthdays are times of celebration. The child who is having a birthday brings cookies for juice time. A small train holding candles is placed in front of the child. As we light each candle, I say:

> This is when you were one year old. You were just beginning to walk. You could only say "Mommie" and "Daddie," and not much more. This is when you were two years old. You could walk and go up and down steps, even run. You could talk and say lots of words. When you were three years old you could even ride a tricycle. You got so you could go to the toilet and not have to wear diapers. You were old enough to go to school. Now you are four years old and you can do almost anything.

We sing "Happy Birthday" and the child blows out the candles and passes the cookies to everybody. We light the candles again and let them burn down before blowing them out and singing again. Birthdays are important because the child is cherished just for being a person. Warmth from everybody comes to the child. It affirms him or her in the group.

Music is inevitably a part of the pulsing of life. It breaks forth from the children spontaneously. When enjoyed, it becomes attached to the core of good feeling in the child. We make up songs like "Ki Yi Yippity" which is sung vigorously with motions.

Ki yi yippity
Ki yi yo .
Come on cowboys
Here we go.

Ki yi yippity
Ki yi yo
Lasso a steer
And don't let him go.

Ki yi yippity
Ki yi yo
Flip a flapjack
And down it goes.

Ki yi yippity
Ki yi yo
Sizzle a steak
And swallow it whole.

Ki yi yippity
Ki yi yo
I'm a cowboy
Ki yi yo.

"Ki yi yippity" is often sung spontaneously when the children are playing cowboy or any other game that gives them a feeling of vigor and freedom. When the children sing "Jingle Bells" it is a sign that they are feeling good about their play. The student teachers bring in their musical instruments to accompany the singing, and the children enjoy it when adults whom they like sing vigorously.

One morning Scott brings a plastic alligator with sharp teeth to school. It is very realistic and some of the children do not want to touch it. At juice time Scott wants to share it with everybody. I can see that some were afraid of it so I take it first.

"He looks very fierce, doesn't he, with those sharp teeth? But he is only a pretend one."

As the children handle it, their comments are very descriptive. That afternoon Mrs. Loehr, the other teacher, writes down their comments and put them to a tune she knows. We sing it the next day.

> He's an enormous alligator.
> He moves his mouth this way.
> He's a strong alligator.
> He likes to play and play.
> He has a long, long, tail,
> And he likes to make it sway.
> He's a fierce alligator
> He likes to snap all day.

We added the appropriate motions and children have enjoyed singing it ever since.

PULSING LIFE

A great deal of living comes at a three-or four-year-old. They have to separate the real from the unreal. The child gets a feeling about people. Each child is ushered into the mysteries of the universe. It can be a wonderful exciting world. It can be a singing world.

Chapter 3

HOW HEALTHY CONSCIENCE DEVELOPS

We are concerned with the growth of a healthy conscience that enables the child to develop potential and live with strength within the human race. Conscience is a central task of the child's nursery school years.

Healthy conscience is basically caring—caring for self that responds to the joy of fully functioning and projecting futures. Caring for others because they too are selves with feelings, intentions, and desires. Such caring comes in the midst of play, and is empowered by skill in understanding others. Conscience enables constructive reconciliation. It anchors the self in humanity.

Healthy conscience commits the self to an honest integrity. It brings about the union of the self. It keeps trying to get together one's behavior and what one thinks is right, so they both are going in the same direction. It continually "trues up" the self and affirms the self when behavior seems right. Such a conscience will not collapse under pressure or warp future growth.

Healthy conscience helps the person transcend what he has done. It opens futures. Conscience is the call of possibility. The nursery school is an optimum place for the growing of conscience and a model for how desirable conscience can develop anyplace.

The growth process in children by which healthy conscience develops is:

1. Caring deeply and understanding others
2. Becoming able to feel, identify, and handle feelings
3. Becoming a personal center and realizing competence
4. Helping establish a justice culture
5. Developing honest inner speech
6. Trueing-up the self
7. Hearing the call to possibility
8. Preferring the highest and best
9. Interiorizing significant adults

These are not steps or building blocks that are placed one on top of the other. They are growth processes, all going on at the same time. Neither are they abstractions to be taught. Feelings, meanings, and thinking are part of the experience.

CARING DEEPLY AND UNDERSTANDING OTHERS

Conscience develops as a child begins to care deeply for someone else.

> Because of tensions in their homes that were beyond the control of the parents, Jill's and Joe's life worlds had become fragile. One morning in December, Jill and Joe both want the doll buggy, a certain doll, and a blanket. Neither of them had played with these toys before.
>
> Joe had been wheeling the buggy with a doll in it around the yard. Jill tells me that she wants it. I tell her that Joe is using it now but that she can get another doll and put it in a wagon and pull it. She does this but then goes directly to Joe.

Jill: "Joe, do you want to pull the wagon?"
Joe: "No."

Jill tries to take the doll and buggy from Joe. They got into a real fight—pulling, crying, and kicking. I put my arm around Jill and get down to talk to Joe.

Mrs. S: "Joe, you want the buggy and the dolly very much."
Joe: (Still crying) "Yes, yes."
Mrs. S: "You like the dolly so much you would like to wheel her around all morning?"
Joe: "Yes."
          (He stops crying.)
Mrs. S: "Joe, Jill likes the dolly too. She would like to wheel her. Joe, you wheel her for five more minutes and then let Jill have a turn."
Jill: "He may have seven minutes."
Mrs. S: "Jill, seven is more than five."
Jill: "Yes."
Mrs. S: "Joe, Jill says you may have seven minutes."

Very pleased, Joe starts off with the buggy. Then he turns around and comes back.

Joe: "Here, Jill, you may have it."
Jill: "That wasn't seven minutes, was it, Mrs. Snyder? He is sort of silly, not taking his turn."
Mrs. S: "No, Jill, Joe wasn't silly. He knows how much you wanted to wheel the dolly. So he is giving you his turn."

Episodes like these reveal what is involved in beginning to care for someone else. The teacher took time to understand what was going on in the situation, and within each child. By communicating this with both children, she let them become part of the effort. Once they understood the meaning of what was going on and felt cared for themselves, they began to care for the other person.

Joe came to understand that the teacher understood how much the doll buggy meant to him. "Joe, you want the buggy and the dolly very much, don't you?" "You like the dolly so much you would like to wheel her around all morning." Once the teacher recognized his feelings, he was free to hear what the teacher was reporting about Jill's feelings and care about them too. The whole process of caring had a rightness about it for him. By hearing Jill's feelings put into words by someone who cares for both of them, he hears and understands her feelings and needs. He begins to see her as a person with feelings and wants. He sees that she suffers as he does. He cares for another self. Jill at the same time understands how much the doll and buggy means to Joe and says, "You may have seven minutes." He is a person, too, not an enemy. To each of them, in spite of their own personal needs, the other child becomes part of his or her life world as a human being. They begin to see each other as persons.

The basis of conscience is the ability to care for another self because that self has feelings.

No one episode, of course, will build a caring conscience; but continued experiences over a period of time do make a difference in the child's feelings about himself and others.

When they enter nursery school, children have various beginnings of a caring conscience. They continue to work on enlarging their caring capacity.

One morning, Dick is taking off his coat in the locker room. He is in a happy mood.

Dick: "My mother wouldn't kill anybody. Not the grocery man, not Ann [his baby sister]. She loves everyone."

Mrs. S: "Your mother wouldn't kill anyone, Dick?"

Dick: "No, she loves everyone. She wouldn't kill Dora and she has a hole in her face. She works for us on the farm. She loves her."

Mrs. S: "Your mother loves Dora even when she has something wrong with her face?"

> Dick: "Yes. She loves her."
> Mrs. S: "It feels good to have a mother who loves every-
>   body?"
> Dick: "Yes."

Dick already showed a great capacity for caring for other people when he entered school. In this conversation he was trying to accept into his caring people who are deformed. A conscience of this kind is the basis for a moral society.

Becoming Able to Feel, Identify, and Handle Feelings

Feelings are the ground out of which caring grows. For some children the starting point in developing conscience is helping the child to feel. Some children are overwhelmed by their feelings because they do not understand them and cannot put them into words. They need help to learn to identify, understand, and act constructively on their feelings.

Faye was quite withdrawn when she entered school. She was a child who could not cry. It took a week for her to gain enough security to move around the room.

One morning, Faye is playing with water in the sink and seems very interested in what she is doing. Other children see her fun and start to play in the sink too. Gradually, Faye is edged out. She drops down on her knees and starts to cry.

> Mrs. S: "You wanted to play in the sink too?"
> Faye: (Still crying) "Yes."
> Mrs. S: "And you wish that you could say to the chil-
>   dren, 'Don't do that. I want to play, too.'"

Faye looked at me with thoughtful eyes, got up, and edged her way back to the sink.

By having words put to her feelings, Faye understood the feelings inside her. She understood what was happening. As a result of our conversation, she also understood that it was all right to want to play at the sink, and that she did not have to let others push her out. She now had words to think and feel with. She could act.

The capacity to feel and understand one's feelings and act on them constructively are necessary components for building a powerful conscience.

Feelings often become intense, and so a child needs help in learning how to handle them. She needs help in processing them so that the total child stays in control of her life and not just the fearful or angry self. (Helping children develop and handle intense feelings is treated in considerable detail in Chapter 6, "Enabling Through the Understanding Mode of Conversation.")

BECOMING A PERSONAL CENTER AND REALIZING COMPETENCE

Conscience develops out of strength, rather than fear and weakness. A "conscienced" person is endowed with energy—the power of inventing and power of resisting.

Conscience is the personal, self-generating center from which this energy flows. It grows as the self experiences doing some things well. To enable a child to function, to do something he or she wants very much to do, is an important function of a significant adult.

Toby was a weak three-year-old when he started school. At first Toby played alongside the other children within his own world. They did not feel they were playing with him. When things didn't work out his face would go blank and he would cry loudly.

On the third week of school he arrived wearing an expensive cowboy hat, a brown plaid shirt, and boots. All of the children admired them.

Toby: "I'm a cowboy, Mrs. Snyder. See, I'm a cowboy."

He rode around the room on an imaginary horse. New feeling tones came into Toby. The cowboy took possession of him and he lived this for several weeks. But his strong cowboy identity and feeling tones sometimes got him into trouble.

One morning Jack is building a house with blocks. Jack tells Toby not to build on his house. Toby hits Jack in the face with a block. Jack starts to cry.

Mrs. S: "Hey, Toby, Jack asked you not to build on his blocks."
           (When Toby sees Jack cry, it disintegrates him. He starts to cry, and big tears roll down his face.)
Mrs. S: "Toby, you wanted to build with Jack, and when he wouldn't let you, you hit him?"
Toby: "I wanna. I wanna."
Mrs. S: "Toby, when things go wrong, you don't know what to do?"
           (He is still crying.)
Mrs. S: "Toby, that is what nursery school is for, to learn how to play together."
           (He stops crying and seems to be listening.)
Mrs. S: "Toby, you are learning how to play with other people."

Toby was beginning to play more freely now with the boys. He was not withdrawing behind a blank mask anymore. But he still had some things to learn that would take him into a new level of relationship. Rather than calling his attention to what was wrong with him, he needed help in understanding the positive task he was working on—learning to play constructively with others.

Toby: "Bang! Bang!"
Mrs. S: "Toby, that was too loud. No guns, you know, at school."
Toby: "That boy [pointing at Jack] told me to stop my silly talk. So I shot him."
Mrs. S: "You didn't think that your talk was silly, and you didn't know what to do?"
Toby: "No, I wasn't talking silly so I shot him."

Mrs. S: "Toby, you could have said, 'I don't think that what I said was silly.' "

Toby: "No, I wasn't being silly."

Mrs. S: "You were wanting to play with Jack and you didn't like having him say you were silly."

Toby: "No, I wasn't silly."

On another morning Willis comes to me rubbing his face.

Willis: "Toby kicked me."

Mrs. S: "Toby kicked you in the face, and it hurts, Willis?" We better go talk to Toby. Toby, Willis says you kicked him in the face and it hurt very much."

Toby: "He kept getting in the way of my stagecoach and he wouldn't stop."

Mrs. S: "You were playing stagecoach, and Willis was bothering your stagecoach?"

Toby: "Yes, and I kicked him with my boots."

Mrs. S: "Toby, it hurt Willis when you kick him in the face with your boots. If you would tell Willis real loud about the stagecoach, I'm sure he would not bother it."

In about 10 minutes, Jim is having trouble. I go to see what is the matter.

Mrs. S: "Jim, somebody hurt you?"

Jim: "Toby kicked me."

Toby: "He kept eating my mouse, and I didn't want him to."

Mrs. S: "You didn't want him to eat your mouse?" (Toby had been playing kitten with imaginary mice.)

Jim: "He didn't have to kick me."

Mrs. S: "It hurt a lot to get kicked, Jim?"

Toby: "He wouldn't stop eating my mouse."

Mrs. S: "Toby, it was your mouse, and you didn't want him to eat it. You need to tell him out loud so he can understand, then no one will get hurt. I don't let other people hurt you, and I can't let you hurt other people."

Later than morning, Toby comes and sits on the green box next to me.

Toby: "Mrs. Snyder, when I make someone cry, it makes me cry, too."

Mrs. S: "You don't mean to hurt them, Toby?"

Toby: "No, I don't mean to hurt them. When I hurt them and they cry, it makes me cry."

Mrs. S: "You cry too, Toby, when you make someone else cry."

Toby: "Yes, I cry too."

Mrs. S: "You don't mean to hurt people, Toby?"

Toby: "No, I don't want to hurt them."

Mrs. S: "But when you are learning to play with other people, sometimes they get hurt. But you don't mean to hurt them?"

Toby: "No, I don't mean to hurt them."

Toby's energies had come into focus. He had become an individuated center. At the beginning of the term he had wanted to be strong and powerful. The cowboy suit helped him get into action, but it got him into trouble with other active children. As he learned skills of relating and playing, his imagination became active. Children began to like to play with Toby. He gained competence, and in the process he acquired conscience.

Caring is not taught, it is first experienced. The child who knows adults only as feeders and givers, knows a limited type of caring. Being enabled to function, to realize competence and the ability to live with others, gives caring a deeper dimension. The adult that does not enable children to grow can only coerce them.

HELPING ESTABLISH A JUSTICE CULTURE

A Justice Culture exists when one life world is in healthy relationship with other life worlds, and when each is becoming better able to function as a person. Certain ways of justice become established, and any child can appeal to them if he feels violated.

The Child and Teacher Form a World

A Justice Culture begins when the teacher and the child establish a world together. Before school starts I visit each child in his or her home. This is important because I am entering the child's life world for the first time and I want our meeting to be in the place where he or she is the most secure. I will be entering the child's world often in the school, in his happy experiences and in his conflicts or fears as he is learning to play and have fun with other children. I want him to experience that I do care for him, that he can trust me, and that I am an interesting person.

I want each child to feel that coming to school opens up new possibilities. So I explain what our school is like, and I tell him that his mother will bring him to school. "We have lots of toys to play with—blocks to build with, cars and trucks, an easel and paints, a sink and water to play with, a housekeeping corner with dolls, dishes, and pans, and we have play dough. Just lots of toys. You may play with anything you want to. If someone else has what you want, just wait a while until they are through with it. If they want it too long, you can tell me and I will help you get a turn. There will be other boys and girls to play with. In the middle of the morning, all of the children go to the toilet. We have juice and crackers to eat. Then we have a rest period. You can put your mat anywhere you want to on the floor. You do not need to close your eyes, just rest and be quiet for a short time. Then we go outside and play with the things out there. We have tricycles, wagons, a sand box, and a big trailer to play in. At 11:30 your mother will come for you, and you will go home and eat your lunch at home, and sleep in your own bed at night, and come back to school the next morning."

When the children arrive the first morning, we start from there, always trying hard to enable each child to function, explaining as we go, understanding feelings when necessary.

Love That Envelops All

Some children come from homes where they have been able to command attention without having to share it with other children. They have been surrounded with a love that centers on them alone. It is a new experience for this child to be in a situation where others are included in an overall love.

> Eileen is a beautiful child. Very quickly she becomes distinguished by frequent crying which she relies on for communication in many situations. Instead of telling people what she wants, she cries. She cries as a way of objecting to what someone is doing; she cries when she feels left out of play; she cries when she feels she is not in control of a developing situation; she cries that people might know she is mad; she cries when she feels she needs help; she cries in order not to remain impotent. At other times she has an ample vocabulary.

Eileen has been warmly attended to by two parents. They had met her needs and showered her with positive attention. Yet she was very immature in her ability to love others. Crying was the way she was accustomed to getting the world she desired in every situation. It was as if she had learned that if she stated "with her guts" that she was victim, the world would immediately come to her rescue and treat her as a princess.

We do not "learn" love merely by being served or loved exclusively. As indispensable as this is, this is not enough. There has to be a system within which we love each other and share love. Such an "enveloping all" love situation is one primordial condition that nursery schools are about.

A Justice Culture in the Process of Becoming

Being in an established Justice Culture is important to the growth of conscience, but being in a Justice Culture that is in process of being established is even more valuable. When a child is thrust into a group in which the ways of relating and doing things are already established, she may learn to do them because she is supposed to do them that way. Her behavior may not be supported by her feelings. Ways of doing things make more sense when the child has been part of working through situations where the feelings of all were put into words.

When a Justice Culture emerges from a group of active life worlds, it is powerful. Everyone has helped establish it and believes in it. This is the unique opportunity of nursery school.

Building a Justice Culture is an experience-by-experience process in which all kinds of behavior are tried out and have to be worked through.

On the second week of school Barry brings a uke to school. It is a music box that plays when the handle is turned. All the children want to play it, but Barry does not want them to.

Byron: "I won't break it."

So I asked Barry if I could see it and he gives it to me.

Mrs. S: "This is a very nice uke you have, Barry. It has such a pretty tone. You are afraid that someone will break your uke?"
Barry: "Yes."
Mrs. S: "I think that Byron would be very careful with it, if you let him have a turn."
Barry: "Well, OK."

Most of the children had turns with the uke and to each child I explained how concerned Barry was that it did not get broken. After the children had their turns, I took it to Barry.

Mrs. S: "Barry, it made everybody feel good to have a turn with your nice uke. Shall we put it in your locker now?"
Barry: "Yes."

My respecting, and others respecting Barry's property made him feel that we respected him. It made him feel good. He was an expanded self after that and played well with the other children. This experience gave Barry a feeling of what other children were like. The other children also got a feeling of what Barry was like. They could trust each other.

I also was helping Barry and the children understand together how his uke was to be used—how the possessions of others were to be respected. By talking over how much he valued his uke and how to handle something another person values very much, they began to feel they were part of the process of building a Justice Culture.

A teacher is not credible to a child until the child experiences the teacher as a person who is for him and knows how to help him do what he wants to do. Children will not listen until this happens. Some have learned to turn off adults.

> Joe is playing at the small table in the housekeeping corner. He is pouring water from a big bottle into the small cups and dishes and running water onto the table and the floor. He is very busy and is enjoying it very much. On my way to talk to him, I pick up two sponges.
>
> Mrs. S: "Joe, it is fun to pour water. Try to do it so the water doesn't get on the floor. It makes the tiles come up when they get wet. Here's a sponge. I will help you clean it up."
> (We clean it up and I leave.)
>
> In a short time Joe is running the water over the top again.
>
> Mrs. S: "If you like to run it over, let's take it to the sink and you can run it over as much as you like."
> (I help him carry the dishes to the sink and help him get started playing again.)

I was enabling Joe to function. He was doing what he wanted to do in a way that fit into the school. He was experiencing me as one who would help him. He could believe in hearing me.

Some children have angry feelings and want to hurt others. These feelings have to be worked out experience by experience. If a child starts to throw sand while playing in the sandbox, I say, "It is fun to throw sand, Bob, but the sand might get in somebody's eyes. It hurts very much if it gets in the eyes." This kind of reply is usually enough for most children. However, the hostile acting child may need more help, so I try harder to help him understand: "It is fun to throw sand, Bob. I wish we could throw sand. But it may get into other people's eyes and that hurts." If the child continues, I act to stop his destructive play and to protect the other children.

> Mrs. S: "Bob, do you want to play in the sand?"
> Bob: "Yes."
> Mrs. S: "If you want to play in the sand, you can't be throwing sand. It might hurt someone."

This puts the decision back upon the child. You hope this will be enough, because you do not want to use force. But if he continues to throw sand, I will say, "Bob, you will have to get out of the sandbox now. You will have to stay out of the sandbox until I am sure you will not throw sand."
I lift him out of the sandbox if he does not get out. If he really loses his control, I may need to sit down beside him until he gets his anger released and he has calmed down.

What I am trying to do is to help him face a moral structure that does not allow a child to violate others or control the whole world. One of the ways conscience develops in the child is to meet an integrity a child likes who represents the constructive values of society.

With Bob I was enacting a to-be-internalized-conscience. At the same time I repeatedly gave him the opportunity to take responsibility for his own behavior. I did not punish him, because that probably would have made him very angry at me, and would have distracted him from the real issue of using sand safely.

When a child wants to hurt others, it is a sign that he does not feel good about himself and needs help in restoring respect for himself. In extreme cases it may be necessary to hold the child when he has lost control. I sit down and hold him so that he cannot hurt others, but not to punish him. If the child is held without the intent to punish him and is given time to work his anger through without scolding or further provocation, there is self-healing and a return to happy functioning. I release him when his anger has been discharged, and then he can return to normal activities, or he may want to enjoy the warmth of a hug.

As the days pass, feelings of what is right are formulated. The ways of doing things make sense and are accepted as being right.

Freedom to Make Decisions

In a Justice Culture children experience the freedom to make decisions, to defend their integrity and meet other persons' integrities, to stand up for justice for someone else, and to experience themselves as a power with people.

Free choice is essential if a child is to help establish a Justice Culture. When children bring toys from home I always enjoy the toy with them. Then I ask if she has brought it for other children to play with or just for them to see. If she has only brought it for people to see, after we have looked at it, I say, "Let's put it in your coat locker in the hall where it will be safe." This is an honest decision I let children make. I never force a child to share things she brings from home against her will. The children become quite free in sharing their personal treasures and it becomes right to them and part of the Justice Culture. They enjoy showing others how their toys work.

> One morning, Adeline brings her new tricycle with a basket, bell, and horn. It is a beauty. During the first part of the morning she takes it out into the school yard. Dick sees it and asks if he could ride.
>
> Adeline: "My father says not to let boys ride."

Mrs. S:	"You don't want boys to ride your bike. You are afraid they might break it?"
Adeline:	"Yes."
Mrs. S:	"Dick likes your bike very much." (I give her time to think.) "You remember how happy you were when he let you ride his two-wheeler?"

She smiles, but cannot get off her new bike.

| Mrs. S: | "If you don't feel that you want others to ride your bike, let's put it by your locker." |

She agrees, and we put it away. After rest period she comes to me.

Adeline:	"I want Dick to have a turn on my bike."
Mrs. S:	"I think it will make Dick feel good to ride your new bike."
Adeline:	"Here, Dick, you can have my bike."

Adeline was allowed to do her own inner struggling until it was her decision. I tried not to make her feel guilty when she would not share her bike. I wanted the decision to come from her own feelings. It is true that she was under some pressure to share if she wanted to use her bike at all. It would have been a serious mistake to agree that only her friends or only girls could use the bike. This would have destroyed the Justice Culture. An artificial, privileged group of persons would have been created who, because of their possessions and friendship, could enjoy things denied to others. They would have been given the power to hurt others and set up destructive rivalries.

Even though I value sharing, and the children begin to know this, it is important to have sharing come from their own wealth of feelings. If one relies on praise to teach sharing, a teacher may be only encouraging a child to please adults. This does not help form conscience, since the perception of another's feelings is absent and the experience of caring has not been developed. Further sharing is less likely to occur when adults are not present.

Helping a child make decisions is part of building an active conscience. The decisions have to be ones that the child is equal to making. The consequences have to be within a child's tolerance range.

Finally the child shares because he cares for others and is attracted by the possibility of play, rather than because the teacher keeps enforcing the principle of sharing.

Defending One's Integrity

When a teacher helps a child defend his integrity and come through so that he feels good about himself, she helps the growth of conscience.

> One morning, the children pick dandelions and put them in paper cups with their names on them. Clark gets into a pushing fist fight with Willis over a cup of dandelions. Both are in earnest, fighting for their rights.

Mrs. S:	"Hey, wait up."
Clark:	"These are mine."
Willis:	"They are not. They are mine."
Mrs. S:	"Wait, let's look and see whose name is on the cup. Clark, it says that these belong to Willis. See, W-I-L-L-I-S."
Clark:	"No, that spells Clark."
Mrs. S:	"Clark, you feel that this cup looks like yours?"
Clark:	"Yes."
Mrs. S:	"Let's find the one that has your name on it, Clark." (We did.)
Clark:	"That's not mine."
Mrs. S:	"The other one looks more like the way you remembered yours looked?"
Clark:	"Yes."

And the episode was over.

Both boys felt good about themselves and each other after this episode. In a Justice Culture, it was right for them to defend themselves. A child needs to feel good about being able to maintain his integrity. A Justice Culture requires that the fair thing be done, but does not force the young offender to admit he was wrong or lying. The fact that W-I-L-L-I-S does not spell Clark was not as important a way to take hold of the situation as recognizing Clark's strong desire to have the cup that looked like his.

Standing Up for Justice for Someone Else

Being able to defend one's own personhood is an important step toward developing a conscience. But a conscience also has to include standing up for the rights of others. In a Justice Culture, somebody will see that a person is not mistreated.

Bob is at low ebb, exhibiting a great deal of hostility. He has worked long at making an elaborate building out of blocks, so when put-away time comes I warn Bob and tell him we will leave his building until last. Clark, Cliff, Marie and Clarise are helping put away the blocks. Clarise picks up some of Bob's blocks by mistake. Bob jumps up and pushes Clarise so hard that she falls against the window. Then he goes to Marie and knocks her down. Cliff, Clarise, and one of the other children start after Bob. Marie gets up and tackles him. Bob starts to cry. He seems frightened.

Mrs. S: "Just a minute, Cliff and Clarise."
          (I shield Bob.) "You saw Bob knock Clarise against the window and push Marie down. You didn't want him to hurt them. Bob, you didn't want them to take down your building. I had told you that we would leave it up till last. When they all started to come after you, you didn't know what happened."
Bob: "No."

> The episode seemed over. The children stood looking at each other.

This was a good healing experience for Bob. The children who were defending justice understood. It caused good feeling in the whole group. When children come to respect and stand up for others, they often feel this way about other forms of life. Van was acting on such a feeling when he told the neighbor boy, who wanted to pull leaves off the tree to fill the wagon that "leaves are the tree's lungs" and suggested they could fill the wagon with rocks.

Power-With

"Power-with" others—in contrast to "power-over" others, or through submission to others—is an important component of an active, potent, desirable conscience. And it is a basis of a justice culture.

The four-year-old girl who approaches another child with the remark (either to herself or to the other child), "I can do that better than you can" is at the moment devoid of conscience. She is trying to establish power-over, to place herself as queen of the castle, rather than experience power-with the other girl. She has internal tensions and needs that prevent her from relating directly with another child.

She needs many experiences of successful joint enterprises that will help her with an honest appraisal of herself and allow her to appreciate the achievements of others.

> Myra is watching three-year-old James climb high in the tree in our nursery school yard. She watches from the ground.
>
> | | |
> |---|---|
> | Myra: | "I can climb higher." |
> | ST: | "You would like to climb too, Myra? Just start up the ladder." |
> | | (Myra climbs part way up but did not get as high as James.) |
> | Myra: | "This is as high as I can go." |

ST: "You have gone as high as you can go and James
       has gone as high as he can."
       (They both stay and enjoy being in the tree talk-
       ing together.)

Now Myra could enjoy being in the tree with James. She did
not have to worry about who was doing better.

A power-with conscience has to be supported by good
feelings that are earned in the give-and-take of relationships. It
is being able to say, "Boy, that was fun," after being together
with friends.

A strong, potent conscience comes from experiences of
having your ideas accepted and extended by others, from the
delight of entering into an adventure thought up by someone
else, and from yelling with, protesting, shouting at, wrestling
with, arguing with, being silly with, taking turns with, defending with, and protecting. Such experiences are the ground of a
power-with conscience.

A Justice Culture requires that all individuals are powerful. A conscience is pitifully weak unless the power-with component is livingly there. A weak conscience is a constant
invitation to disaster. It takes a strong conscience to stand up
against the stupidities and destructiveness that try to take over
almost every arena of our common life. Just a sense of right and
wrong does not make an adequate conscience. Without crucial
experiences of power with valued persons, we are still fearful.
We continue to have attacks of a biting conscience that tries to
macerate us to pulp, to reduce us to zero, and so prevent
healthy conscience from operating exuberantly and effectively.

DEVELOPING HONEST INNER SPEECH

Inner speech is the processing equipment of conscience. A
person uses inner speech to talk to himself and to govern his
conduct. Its primary function is to influence the self rather than

other people. Without inner speech there is no personal appropriation of knowledge. It is one of the developmental tasks of being human.

Inner speech has its beginnings in early childhood. A child begins to talk by using the crucial words of the people around him. He talks to get what he wants. He also talks to communicate his feelings to other people. Every time he talks he is also listening to himself.

As he becomes more aware of himself as an identity, he talks directly to himself, not trying to communicate to anybody else at the time. He uses this speech to present to himself how he feels about what is happening and what he intends. This inner speech enters into the foundations of his identity and determines his mode of relationship to other people.

In the first stages of inner speech the child talks to himself out loud, but later the language is silent. It was once thought that the child's early inner speech, which was called egocentric speech, disappeared around the age of four or five. Then Vygotskii discovered that early inner speech did not disappear, but went inside to become the method by which the person talks to himself.

In the beginnings of inner speech, the child not only vocalizes the words but needs to feel that someone is listening to him. However, he does not expect any interruption or reply from them. He is talking to and building up his personal "sanction center," which gives sanction to what he is doing and thinking. This sanction center can quickly become too limited to just his own intentions. To be healthy, this center must always involve the sense that he is talking not only to himself but to a Justice Culture.

The nursery school deals with the child at the opportune time when inner speech is emerging and acquiring form and content. The child has not yet differentiated his inner speech from the words he speaks out loud to others. He still talks out his feelings and perceptions. And you can hear him in motion.

Some inner speech is person-destroying. It does not join the child with other people—instead it becomes divisive. Perceptions get warped by unmet needs, so the child's thinking and language become distorted. The child's desire rules and seeks immediate gratification. The adult can help him discover what his iṇ ner speech is really saying, and how it is violating and getting him out of touch with what he most fundamentally wants: to be in relationship and to function wholeheartedly.

At the beginning of the school year, some children's communication to others and to themselves takes the followng forms:

Child's Words	Hidden Sanctions
"But I want it."	It is all right to take it away from anybody by whatever means.
"I don't like Tom."	Tom is doing what I want to do. I have a right to stop him.
"It is mine."	I don't have to let others use it.
"I am bigger than Jim."	It's all right to belittle others because I am superior and they are inferior.

If remarks like these continue, they enter into the identity formation of the child. He hears himself saying them out loud and to himself. They become part of his self-image of who he is and therefore must be. His identity becomes fixated making it difficult for him to change or enter into a caring relationship.

The way a person defines his needs and the life situations he faces determines how he will seek to solve them and how he will relate to others. Contrast, for example, the child who says to himself, "How can I control this person?" or "How do I prove I am better than these others?", with a child who says to himself in inner speech, "How can I relate to this person so that we can have fun?" Inner speech is always busy formulating the questions that have to be answered.

In the nursery school years, while inner speech is being formed, children are establishing strategies for relating to others and for being what they think is a desirable self for them. To begin with, these are often strategies for maintaining themselves as they are. One little girl's persistent inner speech tells herself that "In all situations I must be cute. Then the adults will notice and treasure me." Another's strategy is that "If I can't have my way, I will scream and cry. Then they will have to give me what I want." One boy's inner conversation tells him that "If I join the 'good guys', it's OK to hurt the 'bad guys.' "

Inner speech does not usually consist of sentences. Often it is not so much a string of words as it is blobs of diffuse meaning, a geyser of feeling hunting for words to express it.

Often the most basic meaning is symbolized in partly hidden and complex forms. Sometimes it comes out in very direct language.

When Clyde comes up to a little girl and says, "I'm going to hit you and knock you down," he is meeting his need to feel powerful. If he succeeds, he will say to himself, "Isn't it great to be strong? Now I am Superman."

When he comes to where Van is playing and takes over the camper, he is saying to himself in unformulated words, "I must be the kind of person who can control other people." When Clyde finally asks himself, "How can I play with Van?", his inner speech has changed and his identity is changing. Playing with Van is emotionally more satisfying than being a lonesome Superman.

Inner speech is a mode of establishing and maintaining identity. It is more than abstract thinking. Inner speech is continually wrestling with the decisions and actions of the person. It keeps the self working on the basic questions of living: What do I see happening here? What do I really want?

In the episode of Joe and Jill (pages 49–50), Joe gave the doll buggy that meant so much to him to Jill because his own inner speech could present her feelings to himself while he was interacting with her. A new level of relationship was possible, and a new bit of inner speech began.

How important it is, then, to help a child at this early age to care deeply for another self because that self has feelings like he has? This understanding feeds into the child's inner speech and into his system of meanings. If these are caring-for feelings, the conscience will be humane.

Inner speech is the processing equipment of conscience. The quality and range of this early inner speech is crucial.

TRUEING-UP THE SELF

We have presented conscience as caring for other people, having feelings and being able to handle them, becoming a personal center and realizing competence, participating in building a Justice Culture and developing honest inner speech. We now turn to the sixth component of conscience. When being a part of a Justice Culture makes sense, children form and re-form themselves. They begin to "true-up" the self, to correct themselves.

Basically, all children want to live in relationship. They want to function fully. They do not enjoy being scared, timid, or hostile. Often their impulsive or angry behavior gets in their way and has to be worked through.

One morning Jane's mother says good-bye to her three times. Jane does not answer. Then her mother leaves.

Mrs. S: "Jane, you didn't say good-bye to your mother this morning."
(Inviting her to look at her behavior rather than accusing her)

Jane: "I didn't say good-bye to her. I won't say good-bye."
(Very emphatically, stamping her foot)

Mrs. S: "You didn't feel like it this morning?"

Jane: "No! She yelled at me and I *won't* say good-bye."

Mrs. S: "You don't like having people yell at you?"

Jane: "No."

> Mrs. S: "Jane, you know when mothers have children and work too, they have more than they can get done."
>
> Jane: "I know. I wouldn't get dressed and wouldn't eat my breakfast."
>
> Mrs. S: "When mothers have more than they can do, they are apt to get cross."
>
> Jane: "I know."

This is helping a little girl work through her feelings so that she can true-up herself. She was now in charge of her feelings instead of her feelings being in charge of her. If I had moralized, it might have made her feelings tighter. Then she would probably have gone into the morning feeling sorry for herself on a false basis.

Jane had a conflict going on inside her. She did not really want to be at odds with her mother. Rightfully, she was mad at being pushed around. She needed someone to help her work through this conflict. Jane arrived at the place where she could say to herself, "I caused the trouble this morning, not my mother. I would not get up and eat my breakfast." She was developing honest inner speech. In the process of reliving her morning with me, she was able to recover and once more be the girl she likes to be. She did her own changing.

A conscience is in constant struggle to bring one's actions and feelings into union with one's better self. Conscience is the power to search and to find the authentic self.

HEARING THE CALL OF POSSIBILITY

The conscience of a caring person does not have to live by rules and regulations or by habit; but can respond to the human situation. There can be an immediate freshness about a person who responds this way.

> During singing time on the last day of school, the children are asking us to sing their favorite songs. In the midst of the singing, Tilly speaks up.

Tilly:	"Will you sing "Happy Birthday" to me?
Louise:	"Is it your birthday?"
	(Hopefully)
Dick:	"She just wants us to sing it to her."
	(We sing "Happy Birthday" to Tilly.)

Even though it was not her birthday, Dick sensed Tilly's feelings and felt how much it would mean to her. Everybody felt good about singing to her, so we sang "Happy Birthday Everybody". It seemed so right that they wanted to sing it again, so we did.

Preferring the Highest and Best. Truth-Work

Conscience is loyalty to the highest and best we know. In a Justice Culture, when children begin to care deeply, they are fast to choose the better over the destructive.

On the morning after the death of Martin Luther King, Clark came directly to me when he arrived at school.

Clark:	(With concern)"Mrs. Snyder, you know they killed Dr. Martin Luther King last night!"
Mrs. S:	"Yes, some mean people shot and killed him."
Barry:	"They killed him dead, and he is really dead, isn't he?"
Mrs. S:	"Yes, he is really dead."
Charles:	"But why?"
Mrs. S:	"Dr. Martin Luther King was trying to help black people. He was trying to help all people."
Charles:	"But why did they kill him?"
Mrs. S:	"Some people did not like what he said, and what he wanted to do. So they killed him to stop him."
Ben:	"But they shouldn't have killed him."

In spite of all the violence on TV, the children were sure that this definitely was not right. They were upset that a good man had been killed for being good. They had found something to be true to that extended beyond our group. They were being true to the struggling personness in all mankind. They began to see that the world has better and worse in it, that everything does not have the same value, that one action is not as good as another. Conscience enables the person to discriminate and to choose relationship with the highest and best.

"Truth-work" is the effort to live in relationship with the highest and the best. It has two dimensions. It is an open and constructive way of moving toward others so that potential is realized. It is also the inner process of thinking over what is happening in light of what one believes and intends, so that one's own personal truth is actualized.

Inherent in the concept of truth-work is the recognition that there is a moral structure to life, to individual and social actualization. This is in contrast with some thinking on self-actualization which opposes any restraint on personal freedom, and, believing all value to be relative, urges us to accept all choices as equally valid.

Nursey school, being a Justice Culture that is on the side of healthy growth, cannot accept all values and actions. Bullying, stealing, destroying what others are building, and scapegoating can never be accepted as valid ways of treating people. Such behavior clearly destroys the Justice Culture, hurts people, and frustrates the creative process. Freedom is not a license to "do your own thing." It is only within our understanding of the highest and the best that self-actualization takes on direction and significance.

Knowing that there is a highest and a best, a person becomes aware that positive potential exists in all relationships. Since we do not know for sure what form it will take, we must be open to the movement toward truth and creativity within all children. Together we can discover what is best and work to bring it off. Truth-work is therefore a cooperative enterprise made possible by an open and constructive approach to others that intends significant and creative accomplishment.

Truth-work is also the inner process of constructive reasoning that distinguishes the human from the slave or robot. When Toby (pp. 53–56) talks about crying when he hits others, he is doing truth-work. He is reasoning about what his hitting others does to himself and his most basic value of maintaining friendship with others. His truth is to be creative friendship with others, and hitting them destroys this truth. He is reasoning about himself and working to find a way to handle his anger and frustration that does not destroy his positive relationship with others.

Involving children in the process of thinking-through and creating-with others in the light of our knowledge of the highest and the best is a fundamental method for the nursery school.

INTERIORIZING SIGNIFICANT ADULTS

Some of the content of conscience comes from interiorizing the people we admire, people we think attractive, and people who function the way we want to. Parents are significant and their influence lasts a lifetime. The nursery school teacher is a crucial source in the beginning of the development of conscience. If the child experiences the teacher as one who cares for him, is interested in his growth, enables him to function, and seems to know how to do things, that teacher becomes a significant adult in the child's conscience formation. Conscience comes to us in the form of persons.

HOW THIS APPROACH DIFFERS FROM SOME OTHERS

We are primarily concerned with healthy conscience formation, not with using any method that promises immediate results. Well-intentioned adults often feel that punishment or criticism is successful if it gets children to obey. They do not realize that such methods often encourage children to adopt dysfunctional forms of conscience, and that they actually weaken the self-generating and caring process that healthy conscience is based on. Solving problems with children is not to be based on expediency; but determined by an understanding of how an effective conscience develops.

We understand that guilt has destructive and constructive dimensions. When the self is taught to feel "bad," self-hatred results. When regret after hurting someone leads to corrective action, the quality of personal living improves. We do not agree with approaches that try to get rid of all guilt feelings. An important aspect of guilt is the recognition that we are responsible for what happens and that our actions are to be judged by standards that apply to all people. The self-righteous denial of any obligation to others, the sanctioning of self-indulgence, and the centering of morality upon personal pleasure may reduce or even eliminate guilt, but, it does so at the cost of abolishing healthy conscience.

We are not interested in creating a conscience that cripples people with self-hatred or prevents them from enjoying life. We do not attempt to cause or intensify destructive guilt feelings by shaming, questioning underlying motives, or fixing blame. These tactics only lead to withdrawal, denial of responsibility, fearful conformity, or self-hatred. Nor do we force a child to say "I'm sorry." This makes the child say something that may not be true, and does not help that child understand what has happened, or how they can change. When a child does hurt another, we help that child understand the situation and return to creating with the other child.

The knowledge of cognitive development has greatly increased our understanding of children, but some people have incorrectly understood the relationship between cognitive development and the formation and functioning of conscience.

Piaget describes cognitive development as a process of increasing integration and differentiation that leads to the emergence of new capabilities and increasing understanding. Beginning with simple motor and sensory patterns that are formed and then integrated into more comprehensive cognitive structures, an enduring symbolic representation of the external world emerges. The child no longer exists primarily in a flood of emotions and bewildering confrontations. Later, as the child grows in his or her ability to understand the way the world works, there are important developments in thinking and reasoning. The child moves from thinking that is concrete, animistic, egocentric, or legalistic, to thinking that is truly logical, scientific, abstract, and relational. Cognitive development—(to become an active mind equipped with powers to originate, transform, and impose order on the world)—is the main business of education according to Piaget.

Kohlberg believes that conscience is organized around the dominant moral principle on which a person bases her or his moral reasoning. He postulates that conscience goes through developmental stages. The first and most elementary stage of conscience is organized around the principle of obedience out of fear of punishment. The second reasons on the basis of self-interest, while the third is most concerned with getting praise and approval. The fourth believes in law and order, while the fifth thinks in terms of a mutually beneficial social contract. The sixth and final stage reasons on the basis of a commitment to universal ethical principles. Tests of moral reasoning have been used by Kohlberg to identify which type of conscience a person has. Attempts have been made to move people up the scale by learning about these principles and their application.

Some have concluded after studying cognitive development that the young child, lacking the ability to understand fully and reason logically, is not capable of acting ethically and must be treated differently until all the necessary cognitive processes are fully developed. In reality this is not true. Even very young children spontaneously care about others. They are naturally friendly and honest without being forced, unless they have been dehumanized by adults. They like being treated justly, and at times can live in accord with the highest ethical principles, the very principles they cannot verbally explain.

They can do this because the actions of conscience are not altogether dependent on cognitive development. Conscience is based on the integration of a person's experienced understandings of "self" and "world" into a "self-in-world." This bonding of self and others determines how experience is interpreted, meanings formed, and decisions made, and what strategies of relationship are adopted. Since conscience is built on this relationship, approaches that attempt to create conscience through teaching beliefs or moral principles, and approaches that stress training in logical reasoning or that use values clarification, are basically ineffective. They may add to a person's knowledge or understanding of various situations, but they do not change the structure of conscience. They do not alter a person's perception of self or world, nor do they increase that person's interpersonal skills. Belonging and bonding, not logical ability or intellectual knowledge, enable moral development.

A number of current techniques encourage adults to bring up children without "the human connection." These approaches to children share the defects of a contemporary mind whose dead ends are becoming evident: a rootless individualism looking out for its own advantage, its own pleasures, its freedom to express hostility—and a concentration on technology rather than on the humanities. Their concept of person is too small and too partial.

One approach is the idea that leaving children alone and not "interfering" will allow them to learn to solve their problems and to realize a sound morality. This rationalization is often used to justify adult laziness. At its best, it produces a custodial or baby-sitting service. At its worst, it creates a dog-eat-dog environment. We cannot assume that children can discover what is important for them in a vacuum where adults hold themselves aloof. Nor can children choose what they have not experienced.

We believe that children need to encounter adults as a presence, as people with enthusiasm with whom they can co-create as people who care deeply, understand, and have fidelity to their personhood and the making of a Justice Culture. Such encounters with interesting and exciting people are interiorized, and this mode of moving out toward people becomes one of the relational strategies of conscience.

The reliance on ideology and logic is another such technique. We have only to look at the human disasters of the twentieth century to see that extremely rational and coherent ideologies were capable of systematically destroying or degrading large numbers of people. The critical question then becomes deciding the purpose to which we are going to apply our reason. Encountering others and participating in the creation of a Justice Culture are necessary for the belonging and bonding that tie reason to humanity.

A third widely used technique consists of behavioral modification and behavioral contracting. These are capable of teaching behavior and give children incentives to make progress. Learning theory helps us realize the importance of paying appropriate attention to children. But, as with logic, we must look at what it intends to accomplish and at what it does to the conscience. If compliance is the goal, we adults become behavioral technicians who control rewards and manipulate desired responses. If personhood is the goal, encountering each other as persons, sharing enthusiasms, caring for, understanding, being an integrity with, and co-creating become our method. The difference between the conscience formed and the type of personal existence encouraged by these two approaches is very significant.

Since we find the integration of the self and world to be the primary determinant of conscience, we conclude that conscience selects the ethical principles to be used, rather than vice versa. If we believe, with Kohlberg, that conscience is controlled by ethical principles, it is hard to explain how the same person, with a specific type of conscience, acts differently at different times or in different situations. If conscience is based on an integration of self and world, such differing actions can be understood. When a child feels valued and experiences the world as a safe and interesting place, behavior consistent with the higher ethical principles may result. When a child feels despised and rejected and experiences the world as dangerous, then behavior motivated by fear, selfishness, or anger is more likely.

We do not understand conscience to grow in a series of quantum leaps from one ethical principle to another; nor do we believe that development always moves to more effective forms of conscience. Conscience becomes more stable, consistent, and moral as a person's understanding of his own worth deepens, his competence with others increases, his understanding of the world is more insightful, and his awareness of the ground that constitutes "self" and "other" frees him from being controlled by external events and social pressures. We shall explore this concept of the child as a "worlding self" in some detail in the next chapter on Life World.

In addition to understanding how healthy conscience may be facilitated, it is often necessary to understand the dysfunctional conscience. It is built on a different integration of self and world, with different relational goals. Understanding this, the teacher is better able to work with a child who has this kind of conscience. Furthermore, the teacher can evaluate proposed methods for being with children. She can avoid in her own teaching those actions that promote dysfunctional and self-limiting forms of conscience.

Self-Limiting and Destructive Consciences

The punitive conscience is an attempt of a frightened and endangered self to cope with a hostile and destructive world. Such a conscience is based on fear and is primarily concerned with avoiding punishment or, when it has been hurt, with getting revenge by hurting back. The cry of the biting, condemning conscience is, "Don't do that. If you do, you must be hurt." Lying, blaming others, and self-deception are necessary to avoid or reduce punishment and guilt. Justice is understood as punishment or getting revenge. It is devoid of compassion or reconciliation. Passive conformity occurs in the presence of others possessing superior power; oppression and exploitation occur when others are weaker.

The paranoid-pessimistic conscience is more interested in maintaining a paranoid world-view and using the identity of an "innocent and helpless victim" to excuse its own behavior than in taking initiative to live constructively with others or in handling injustice effectively. It is built on socially sanctioned self-deception. Personal responsibility for what occurs is denied and innocence is defended: "I didn't do anything; it was their fault." Others are frequently provoked. When they respond appropriately, unfair persecution is alleged. Fear of losing self-esteem, or fear that rage will become uncontrollable in response to frustration, causes the paranoid-pessimistic conscience to conclude: "It is better not to try; it will never work." Constructive effort is abandoned and finding a scapegoat is necessary to discharge rage at being impotent and to build up self-esteem.

The other-directed conscience integrates a weak, dependent self and a world that is believed capable of providing satisfying nurture. The directives of this conscience are, "Don't do anything that might cause others to reject you; be sure to please those who can give you what you want." Praise is sought, and disapproval or rejection is feared and avoided. Conformity is the primary mode of being but destructive jealousy and competitiveness may erupt when nurture is threatened. Because the person lacks an independent integrity, creative self-actualizing energies are suppressed and there is no strength to stand up against injustice affecting oneself or others.

The exploitive-opportunistic conscience uses the world for what it wants. It asks, "What's in it for me?", and follows the primary directives "Me first" and "Do your own thing." What is needed is taken, what is desired is used irresponsibly. The rights and opportunities of others are disregarded. Stealing, bullying, arrrogance, defiance of legitimate authority, refusal to acknowledge responsibility or enter into commitment, and a self-deceiving sense of persecution are manifestations of such a conscience.

The disconnected conscience seeks to program a poorly integrated and poorly understood self with other people's "wisdom." It is unable to put into action what it says since its beliefs are disengaged from the power that runs the self. Such a conscience is actually a "pretended conscience," consisting of misunderstood words, spurious reasoning, and nonproductive routines rather than fullness of heart and mind and strength. Ethical principles that have been learned by rote or programmed in by outsiders are uncreatively adhered to, rigidly followed. They are often used to hide ulterior motives and to deceive others. The creative life, denied to the self, is also denied others. This conscience says, "Conscience is something that can be given to me. I'm not involved in its development, nor expected to live what I say I believe."

How the Self-Limiting and Destructive Consciences Come About

Children form a conscience that can best cope with the reality that faces them and interiorize the behavior modeled by significant adults. They become disciples of the discipline they experience. Therefore the reality that adults create for children and the methods adults use to handle feelings and solve interpersonal problems are of the utmost importance.

When adults intentionally hit, humiliate, degrade, or threaten a child, they make the avoidance of punishment the central concern of that child's conscience. They provide a model of how a punitive conscience operates, and the child will copy and later interiorize. The child's experiential understanding of justice is restricted to punishment and revenge. The child is pushed to develop a biting and condemning punitive conscience and to adopt the behavior that goes along to support it.

The paranoid-pessimistic conscience is a response to being repeatedly thwarted by others and to having significant adults confirm that one is an "innocent and helpless victim" deserving of pity and special treatment. Such adults blindly take the child's side of a conflict, disregard what the child contributes to the problem, encourage a paranoid world view, and do not enable the child to live constructively with others. Encouraging a child to believe he or she is a "victim" is different from giving a child necessary support and protection where he or she is overwhelmed and discriminated against.

Adult reliance on praising children can encourage children to suppress their authentic self and destructively conform or compete for approval. This encourages the development of the other-directed conscience, especially when adults discourage initiative and independent activity. There is a significant difference between recognizing and celebrating a child's own accomplishment, and praising a child for being "good" or doing what the adult has commanded. Adults who get upset when children make just requests, or who discourage children from standing up for themselves when they are unjustly treated because other adults will be upset, train children to become passive and other-directed.

The exploitative-opportunistic conscience is encouraged by adults who believe that children should have complete freedom to do as they please even when it hurts others, violates the Justice Culture, or means breaking commitments and not carrying out responsibilities. This is sometimes compounded when adults identify with children as being unjustly treated or feel sorry for them and excuse them from their responsibilities. Bribing can contribute to the attitude that you do not have to cooperate if you are not rewarded. (bribing has to be distinguished from appropriately rewarding or paying a child for work that has been accomplished.)

Adults also contribute to the formation of such an exploitative-opportunistic conscience by protecting children from the natural consequences of their behavior. This teaches children that they can be irresponsible and that nothing serious will result since someone always benevolently intervenes, unpleasant natural consequences do not occur, and they are always given another chance.

Systems of behavioral training that utilize externally imposed rewards run the risk of encouraging the other-directed or exploitative-opportunistic conscience. Teaching "acceptable" behavior is not the same as enabling the child's own caring. It does not foster the formation of the personal intention to live considerately and constructively.

The disengaged conscience results from attempting to short cut conscience development. Understanding and insight developed by others cannot be superimposed on those who have not gone through the conscience developing process. Working through a problem is a different experience from having the solution given to you. Without coming to care deeply, understand others, and develop power with people, the words and phrases or morality lack personal meaning and the power to motivate.

WHAT HEALTHY CONSCIENCE IS: THE CARING-CONSTRUCTIVE CONSCIENCE

From living with three- and four-year-olds, we have found nine kinds of activity that contribute to conscience development at this age. A person's conscience is all of these contents working together. Conscience is not best thought of as the generalized stages that some theories of conscience and morality have offered for a teacher's use. These nine activities are the functional livingness with which children develop, and of which they can be in charge.

The nine activities we have described and documented in this chapter cohere into three clusters of functioning.

1. *Conscience is appreciative caring.* Conscience is caring that comes from richness of feeling and intention,

understanding the worlding that others are trying to bring off. It is wealth of subjectivity.

2. *Conscience is constructively helping establish a Justice Culture, a Justice Culture in the making.* This has been described here by the concepts of "a love that envelops all," "in the process of becoming," "freedom to make decisions," "defending one's integrity," "standing up for justice for someone else," and "power-with."

3. *Conscience is integrity work.* It is becoming a personal center and a constructive participant in a culture that has a history, an integrity, and a future. This integrity work has been presented here in terms of "becoming a personal center and realizing competence," "honest inner speech," "trueing-up the self," "hearing the call of possibility," "preferring the highest and best," "truth-work," and "interiorizing significant adults."

Richness of feelings and appreciative caring, helping to establish a justice culture, constructive integrity work—these three and their contents are what conscience is and how it grows.

There is an irridescence to this kind of conscience.

"Our shoes are alike."

Chapter 4

A CHILD IS A LIFE WORLD

A child is always organizing a Life World in which he or she lives, and from which the child functions. Out of his encounters with all that surrounds him, the child organizes a uniquely personal world-to-be-lived. This Life World is organized by the growing the child is working on, the projects in his or her imagination, and the meanings of particular actions, persons, and objects.

Every child is a worlding project. He is a Life World trying to realize himself through encountering, incorporating, and making a "world out there" that includes him. He is continually putting together a world to live for the next few minutes, as well as a world that will hold together over a longer time. He is worlding himself.

A child's Life World cannot be given to him by someone else. Each child constructs it from his experiences, his intentions, and the meanings awakened in him. A major function of the nursery school teacher is to help a child learn how to bring off this worlding of himself. For a child and the world have to get together.

ORGANIZING CENTERS OF A LIFE WORLD

We have found the following organizing centers in the Life World of children:

1. The growing the child is working on
2. Feelings about self
3. People and objects in the child's world
4. Method of meeting life
5. Meanings being developed
6. Future

A knowledge of these organizing centers is fundamental in understanding a child. Around these centers clusters much of the content of a child's Life World.

The Growing that the Child is Working On

A child is a trust into life. From the moment the baby is born, she moves her arms, kicks her legs, and explores with her mouth. All systems are go! She starts reaching out into life. Almost immediately, she is working on something. She starts to figure out the tremendous and exciting world of which she is now a part.

To help a child in any particular moment, the teacher needs to discover what the child is working on. And this is not always obvious. Often the child's needs are hidden under false signs like withdrawal or hostility. When she is possessed by these feelings, she exists in a world that is self-defeating. It is not a pleasant world. But the child does not want someone to take over her life. She wants someone who will enable her to function.

Some children's behavior is hard to figure out. It does not make sense until the adult understands the growing that is being worked on.

Bert is a fast-moving three-year-old whose behavior gives conflicting signals. He never hurts other children, but he will take their toys and run to another part of the room before the toys are missed. Often, if he thinks no one was looking, he will break a tóy. In the play yard, he throws toys over the fence after he uses them. His ego strength is good, but he does not play with other children.

At first I thought that Bert had not learned impulse control. But two conversations finally gave me the clue to the growing he was working on.

On a rainy day I take a group of children into the hall to ride on small triangle scooters. Bert is radiant as he races up and down the hall on his scooter. Suddenly he stops.

> Bert: "Mrs. Snyder, you know my brother couldn't do this. He can't run."
> (Bert has a crippled nine-year-old brother who is confined to a wheel chair. He has not talked about his brother before.)
>
> Mrs. S: "No, Bert, your brother is crippled and he can't run and play and have fun like you, can he?"
>
> Bert: "Nick just has to stay in his wheel chair."
>
> Mrs. S: "That is sad, isn't it, that Nick can't run, and that other people have to help take care of him."
>
> Bert: "Yes."
>
> And off he goes to race on the scooter.

The second conversation occurred a few weeks later. The children are in the bathroom at toilet time. One child notices that Woody had a Winnie-the-Pooh button on his pants. The children are admiring it.

> Bert: "I don't have a Winnie-the-Pooh button."
>
> Mrs. S: "You like Woody's button, Bert?"
>
> Bert: (In a longing tone) "I don't have one. But Nick has one on his pants."
>
> Mrs. S: "Your brother seems to have lots of things, Bert?"
>
> Bert: "He has lots of toys."
>
> Mrs. S: "He seems to have more than you, Bert?"

Bert: "Yes, he has lots."
(With much feeling)

Mrs. S: "Bert, you know Nick is crippled and has to stay in a wheel chair all the time."

Bert: "He can't walk."

Mrs. S: "When a person can't walk they need lots of toys to play with."

Bert: "Yes."
(His face has a relaxed softness to it.)

Gradually, Bert's destructiveness disappeared. He could share and enter into relationships with his peers. On his birthday his parents made sure that he received presents that were important to him. He brought his toys to school and shared them with the children. They respected his toys, and good feelings developed in him.

As long as Bert felt that his brother was preferred, his Life World was that of an undesired and rejected self, struggling to protest and get revenge on an unfair world. It affected his whole behavior. His strategy was to break up Nick's toys when no one was looking and to get away fast. This perception and his strategy were blocking his relationships and preventing him from accurately understanding his parents.

Bert was working on his relationship with his mother and father. He desperately wanted to belong and, in his own immature way, he was saying "See me. I am your son too. I really want to be. I need toys. I need love." Nick's getting so many toys had symbolized to Bert that he was not loved. I helped him see that Nick's having toys fitted his needs and handicap. It was not intended to mean that Bert was not loved. His feelings about both his parents and himself changed, enabling him to organize a more constructive Life World.

There is something inside every child that causes him to keep struggling not only to survive, but to fulfill himself and to belong. He keeps working away at it. This need to fulfill himself and be in relationship drives him to continually reconstruct his Life World. When a child is not in relationship, the teacher needs to keep asking herself why. What is blocking the child? The teacher can be most helpful to the child at the point of his present need. Otherwise she keeps responding to symptoms.

> Lloyd is an extremely busy little boy with a bright happy face. He has been on the go from the minute he entered school. If he gets into trouble he will leave that situation and find something else to play with.
>
> At the end of the first week, his mother tells us that Lloyd is very happy about nursery school, but that he comes home exhausted and takes a long nap. Later we learn Lloyd had been sick as a baby. The doctor had put a tube in his brain to drain off fluid so that pressure would not build up and destroy his brain tissue. He also wore special shoes to help his undeveloped foot muscles.
>
> Lloyd had a lot of catching up to do, and he was in a hurry to do it. As soon as we realized the growing he was working on, we could help him with his very inquiring mind. Until we discovered the tremendous effort he was making, our focus had been on how to slow down this boy's driving energy.

The growing that a child is working on is always a significant factor in that child's behavior. It is a constant organizer of his Life World and a stimulus to his activity.

Feelings About Self

A child's feelings about herself also organize her Life World. They dominate the climate and weather of that world.

The feeling-picture of self is always at the center of the world the child puts together to live. When a child feels very bad about herself, she tends to act compulsively, trying to destroy the play or status of another child. Or she draws back, defining herself as weak, undesirable, a victim. She tries to organize a world that sympathizes with her. Her lack of morale leads her to try things half-heartedly. Therefore she fails in the activity. She becomes bored. When it is no longer fun to be herself, the world becomes polluted and suffocating. When her feeling about herself is sick, the whole world is sick. Not loving herself, she can hardly love others. The reverse is equally true. Freed to respect herself, she can put together a world filled with respect.

SELF-VALUING   All experiences leave a memory in the feeling structure of the child. Self-valuing is a composite of the way life has come at a child. It is the child's feelings about the picture she has of herself. It comes from her experiences of being valued by people who are significant to her and from her realization of competence.

> On Friday of the first week of nursery school, Betty comes skipping into the room. I am sitting on the floor and she comes directly into my lap.
>
> Betty: "Smell me, smell me, I don't smell anymore." (She keeps talking breathlessly.)
>
> Mrs. S: (A bit puzzled about why this was important to her) "Betty . . ."
>
> Betty: "I wore my new yellow nightie, I didn't wet my bed, and I don't smell anymore."
>
> I want to say that this is fine and that she will learn to keep her bed dry. But she keeps talking. Already she has put herself against my nose.
>
> Betty: "Smell me, smell me. I don't smell anymore." (She skips off to play.)
>
> Everything went well until the next Friday, when Betty is absent. Her mother explains that Betty had wet her bed again, and she told Betty if she was not old enough to keep her bed dry, she was not old enough to go to school.

What does such treatment do to Betty's feelings of her own worth? One isolated episode may not hurt a child. But if this is the continuing mode of relationship, her picture of herself will gradually become self-depreciating. What might this do to her power to form an energetic Life World? When she enters first grade, will she feel that there is something wrong with her, that fundamentally she stinks?

A child's self-valuing can be a feeling of being weak and inadequate, that other children are better. It can be the feeling that the world is hostile and that the only way to survive is to seize the initiative in hurting. Or it can be a feeling of being capable—a feeling that life is good.

Carl is a three-year-old boy whose picture of himself and feelings about himself changed during the year. At the beginning of school, he was aggressive and loud, he acted strong and tough. But he was actually weak and scared. He seemed to get into lots of trouble. If a child protested and made a big fuss, Carl would back off saying 'I'm sorry," as if this was a sure way out. By spring, because of many successful play relationships, he had discovered that he could trust active boys and hold his own with them. His self-valuing had changed.

One Spring morning, all the children are outside playing while I prepare the table for juice time. Carl comes in and watches. He leans one of his elbows on the table, and speaks in a thoughtful way.

Carl:	"You know, I like this table. I like the chairs. I like the sinks. I like everything about this school."
Mrs. S:	"I'm glad you like our school, Carl, I like having you in our school."
Carl:	"You know, a long time ago I only played with one boy at a time. But that was before I knew this was such a good school."
Mrs. S:	"Now you like to come to school and play with lots of children."
Carl:	"Yes."

Carl had now included all of the children in the school as his friends, and felt good about them. He liked himself. He felt strong.

When a child feels good about himself, he can take a lot of hard falls in stride.

> In the Spring some of the children make kites and take them into the yard to fly them. Carl is very pleased to run with his so that it will fly out in back of him. Then I see him standing on top of the trailer. Holding his kite, he leaps into the air and lands flat on his stomach. His mouth is full of mud and his nose is bleeding. He looks up smiling.
>
> Mrs. S: "Oh Carl! You should always land on your feet."
> Carl: "But I had my kite."
> Mrs. S: "Carl, you did have your kite, but it is not strong enough to hold you up. Even a parachute jumper lands on his feet."
>
> We go in to wash the mud out of his mouth. Then he takes his kite and goes out to play again.
> This was a big contrast to the falls he took when he felt weak, when each little bump set off intense crying.

COMPETENCE AND EGO STRENGTH   Ego strength is closely related to self-valuing. Ego strength is inner power coming from many experiences of "I can," "I am able," and "I am in relationship." Learning to walk, to ride a trike, and to be wanted by friends, brings an inner glow of confidence. Each success adds strength that is available for the next attempted achievement. It enables the child to withstand being hurt many times in the process of trying.

The child who has had freedom to explore when learning to walk is apt to have a sureness about himself. Some children who have been kept in a playpen and slapped when they try to get out are apt to hold back. Others who have been too controlled may have a compulsive need to dominate all situations or to run away from close relationships for fear of being smothered.

Children differ greatly in the amount of ego strength with which they start school.

One Spring morning Robin runs to a student teacher.

Robin: "Look, the baby leaves are coming out and it's
warm, and I'm going to dig worms, and you can
help. And I'm going to play alligator and tiger.
You can be the little . . . no, the daddy tiger."
(And off he goes to begin most anything.)

Here is a boy aware of the world around him, projecting
all kinds of enterprises, reaching out for social relationships.
But a bright child is not necessarily a competent child.

Alvin is a three-year-old boy who is small for his age. He is a
bright boy and speaks two languages, but he cannot play with
other children or with toys. One morning he looks at a small
truck.

Alvin: "The truck is yellow, Mrs. Snyder."
(With no idea of touching it)

Mrs. S: "It is yellow, Alvin, but it can carry big loads of
bricks to build houses. See, like this."
(I build a road with blocks for the truck to ride
on. He watches, but does not touch the truck.)

Alvin had not experienced toys as something to play with.
Pictures of toys had been used to teach him colors. When I called
on Alvin in his home, the spring before he came to nursery
school, we established a good relationship. His mother told me
they had not succeeded at helping Alvin with toilet training, but
she was sure they would have it done by fall.

When school started, Alvin arrived wearing diapers, soak-
ers, training pants, and top pants. He continued to have a bowel
movement in his pants early each morning. The bowel movement was the messy kind that ran down his legs and over his
shoes. It was not the kind you could ignore, particularly in a
group where other children might look upon him as a baby. It
did not bother him. He would tell me after it happened. It took
two weeks to help him learn to have his bowel movement in the
toilet. Soon after he arrived each morning, I would take him to
the toilet.

Mrs. S: "Alvin, let's go to the toilet so you won't have your bowel movement in your pants."
(He goes with me willingly.)

Mrs. S: "Put it in the toilet, Alvin, so it won't get in your pants."

I discovered from experience that he would not have his bowel movement in the toilet the first time I took him. If I would take him again in 15 minutes, he occasionally would do it, but for the most part he would only sit on the toilet and repeat what I said to him but still not do it.

Alvin: "Put the BM in the toilet. Mrs. Snyder does not like to clean up a messy old BM."
(He would laugh but not do it.)

During the rest of these mornings I am especially careful to enable him to do what he wants to do so that he will continue to feel that I am for him and we keep the good relationship we had established.

Finally, one morning he has his bowel movement while on the toilet.

Alvin: "Mrs. Snyder, Mrs. Snyder, look! It's in the toilet."

Mrs. S: "Alvin, you did put it in the toilet! Now you know how!"
(He jumps up and down with excitement.)

The good feeling spread to other activities. That morning he goes to the blocks, builds a road, and starts to play with the trucks. Ego strength comes with each new accomplishment. One day he is struggling with his suspenders.

Alvin: "These old suspenders are a nuisance. They keep coming unsnapped. They get in my way. I can keep up my own pants."

Mrs. S: "That's right, Alvin, you're tired of things getting in your way."

Alvin had very little ego strength when he started school; but given the opportunity—and some help—to take over his Life World, he was able to take control. The more he succeeded, the more ego strength he had for the next step.

IDENTITY   Identity is the discovery a person makes when she says, "I am me. I am unique and valuable. I have a future."

One morning in the nursery school, Ron and Jill are playing Huckleberry Hound and Yogi Bear. At juice time, this conversation takes place.

Ron:	"I'm Huckleberry Hound. I better take off my cowboy hat."
Ron:	(Later, with a satisfied feeling) "Mrs. Snyder, I'm not anybody anymore. I'm just Ron."
Mrs. S:	"It feels good to be Ron, doesn't it? You know, there isn't anybody in the whole world just like you?"
	(He seems pleased.)
Jill:	"And I'm not anybody, either. I'm just Jill. Is there anybody like me?"
Mrs. S:	"No, Jill, there isn't anybody in the whole world like you."

Each child in the nursery school asks if there is anybody like him or her, and each child has to be told there is no one in the whole world that is. After all of them have their turn, I conclude:

Mrs. S:	"Isn't it a wonderful world! There are no two people alike."

Through his or her actions, the young child is continually asking the very crucial questions of life: Who am I? Do you really love me? Do you want me to grow? What kind of person do you think I am? Am I able to do what I want, or am I inadequate? Do I get along with others, or am I disliked? Am I doing the things I should, or am I bad?

Identity also depends on how a child accepts being a girl

or boy. The goal for both girls and boys is for each to feel good about him or herself biologically, and to be free to enter into life equally.

Girls seem to enjoy playing in the housekeeping corner because they have observed their mothers taking care of the house. Some boys need help in accepting that it is all right for them to enjoy taking care of dolls and playing house. Some girls need help in allowing boys to play in the housekeeping corner. At the beginning of the year, the play is apt to be getting meals, feeding and washing the babies. As the boys come into the play, there is a great deal of family play in which different roles are tried out. The play usually includes a mother, father, baby, and sometimes a baby-sitter, a big sister or two, and brothers.

Some girls need to be helped to do more than play in the housekeeping corner and do handwork. Girls have to develop their strength, because this too is part of being feminine. Girls need encouragement to climb, build with blocks, play ball, run, ride a bicycle, play in mud, dig worms, be a doctor as well as a nurse, take turns being the engineer on the train. Some of the names for certain jobs make it hard for a girl.

> Jill: "I'm a cowboy girl."

> Sally: "Give me a hat. I'm going to be a fireman."

Girls should not feel excluded from activities because they are girls.

Some boys need to gain strength in being masculine. It helps a boy to be able to wrestle and hold his own with boys his own age.

> In a sporting way, Jack, the youngest boy in the school, tackles Roy, the biggest and happiest boy, and knocks him down. Roy is surprised; to protect himself he pushes Jack in the face.

Mrs. S: "Jack, you want to play with Roy? Roy, Jack is learning to wrestle. He just wants to have fun. But no pushing in the face."

(Roy understands and they continue. Then Jack, pleased with his success, pushes Roy in the face.)

Mrs. S: "Hey, Jack, no pushing in the face."

(Roy smiles and Jack feels big and they continue to wrestle.)

Boys need to develop and feel their strength. They also need to learn to control it. Further development seems easy to a boy who feels good about being able to hold his own with boys his age. Being able to climb trees and do risky things is ego building. Being competent in anything that rates with the other boys is important. Being good at games and sports provides a feeling of security.

For the weak boy who has a hard time establishing himself with the boys and who gets his emotional security from being near the teacher, becoming a man is not apt to be very attractive. Feeling inadequate as a boy is a weak foundation for becoming a man.

At the end of a morning at nursery school, a man student teacher starts to take sand out of Clark's shoes. Immediately, five other children line up on the sandbox to get the sand taken out of their shoes. Fred is the last to have his done.

Fred: (In a very weak, whining voice) "I'm not going to be a daddy."

ST: "Not ever going to be a daddy, Fred?"

Fred: "No, they have too much to do."

ST: "Daddies have to do too many things, Fred?"

Fred: "Yes."

ST: "Like taking sand out of shoes?"

Fred: "No, like jumping out of windows."

(He seems upset.)

ST: "You didn't like hearing me play the bagpipes in the nursery school this morning, Fred?"

> (The student teacher loses him here by not stay-
> ing with the topic of conversation.)
> Fred: "No, I like the bagpipes."
> (He was very offended)
> "I don't feel like I could be a daddy."
> (Fred starts to walk away.)

Fred was working on becoming a man. He was trying to integrate this into his identity. But unacceptable anticipations were getting in his way. We do not know whether his reference to men jumping out of windows referred to a specific occurrence, a television program, or hearing an overworked father make a complaint that Fred took literally. It must have fit his feelings at the time for it to have been so real to him. The student teacher failed to catch Fred's feelings that fathers are overworked and have no fun, and perhaps do things that are self-destructive. This conversation gave us the clue that Fred needs us to help him build up his ego strength and competence.

Being masculine also means taking part in the necessary work of maintaining a home and taking care of children. We help boys enjoy playing in the housekeeping corner.

We do not encourage or forbid boys to dress up in dresses. Dresses may be attractive to a boy because they have bright colors, are made of soft materials, and can be made into costumes. But encouraging a boy to wear a dress so that he can act out a female identity may lead him to feel that he is not a boy and is preferred as a girl. Some mothers who encourage boys to dress up like girls also prevent them in other ways from becoming masculine. They later get upset and angry when the boy prefers a feminine identity or uses it to upset them.

A boy's identity is partly attached to his penis. The sensitive boy with a small penis is apt to be emotionally hurt by comparisons made by other boys.

> Clark: "Tim's penis is little, but mine is big."
> Mrs. S: "Some boys have big penises, some have little penises. A small penis works just as well as a big one."

When a boy starts bragging about his penis while going to the toilet, I do not want a girl to feel inferior, so I say, "Boys have a penis, girls have a uterus." Since some girls feel inferior because their uterus does not show, I explain, "The uterus is inside so a baby can grow in it and be warm and protected."

Both boys and girls need help in accepting their biological role. The basic personal needs are the same. Each sex needs to be validated. A girl needs to feel good about being a girl. A boy needs to feel good about being a boy. This does not happen simply by telling them so. It is real when—from experience—they feel that it is so.

The People and Objects in the Child's World

Each child selects certain things from his environment and makes them his world. A teacher needs to know what a child is including in that world. What activities does the child participate in? Who does the child play with? Who does he avoid? Why? Which children does the child look upon as helpers in his projects? Which ones does the child regard as obstacles? What playthings are important? What use does the child make of them? What creative imaginings is the child caught up in?

How does he relate to adults? How does he feel about his family and his place in it? How does he accept his brothers and sisters in relation to his father and mother?

A child's definition of his place in his family can be the cause of a great deal of trouble and needs to be dealt with throughout the nursery school year. The trouble usually comes from two sources. The child is not able to do what older brothers and sisters can do, and he or she often gets the feeling of being inferior. A new baby in the family may cause the child to feel displaced in the affections and attentions of the parents.

Some children feel displaced even before the baby's birth. One girl resented the unborn baby because it went to work with her mother. Another girl was looking forward to the baby, but already sensed that the parents wanted a boy. She evidently felt something was wrong with her, since they wanted a boy so much.

> Anabel: "If the baby is a girl, I will tell you, Mrs. Snyder, but if it's a boy . . ."
> (She clenches her fist and shakes it at me.)

Her parents did not realize how deep this feeling was. When the baby boy arrived, Anabel had trouble from the beginning.

Another boy suffered real personal damage during the difficult pregnancy of his mother.

> One day Fred's normal speaking voice is whiny, and even when he yells it remains whiny. His mother is sick and the baby is almost due. Fred has regressed during this period.
>
> Three children are at the table with Fred in the housekeeping corner. The small doll was in the center of the table. Fred picked up the doll and with real excitement in his voice,

> Fred: "Let's eat the baby. I'll eat the head. You eat the leg. You eat the hand."

> The other children continued what they were playing.

> Fred: "Let's eat the baby. I'll eat the head, you can eat the leg. You eat the hand. Let's."

> Nobody joined in this play so Fred did not continue it. This episode could be interpreted many different ways. I believe Fred was trying to get the baby who had caused so much trouble out of the way so that it would not be a bother any more. His voice did not have a mean tone, but expressed real excitement.

After a new baby arrives, the older child often feels that the baby is preferred. The mother is now giving her love and time to the new baby. What was once the child's place in the family is now the baby's. The child has been dispossessed. The caresses are being given to someone else. Feelings of privation and exclusion get mixed up inside. But worst of all, the child's life world has been shattered. Much that held him together as a person has given way, including the trust and dependence on his parents and other people, and even feelings about himself. Many of the child's resources have been demolished. Wanting to hurt back may be a hopeful sign of the child's will to survive. It is wrong to label the child "jealous."

The child must be helped to put together a new Life World. The past Life World is no longer possible. The child needs to feel that he or she is still loved, even if love and care are extended to the new baby. The child's ego strength needs to be restored with experiences that enlarge feelings of competency. Just to be given a new toy to cuddle is not enough. The child's world needs to be expanded. Life needs to open up for the child with a new possibility of a future because the future is a crucial part of any person's Life World.

Often a child with an older brother or sister will identify with the older one when a younger child replaces him or her. This can help the child accept the family's new world. A boy needs to feel that he can become a big brother, and a girl that she can become a big sister. For a child with good ego strength, this is not too great a problem.

However, it is difficult for some three- and four-year-old children who already feel that they cannot do what older brothers and sisters can do. When they try and do not have the same success as the older child, they feel the discrepancy and would rather give up than look like a failure, particularly when a new performance level is thrust upon them. A four-year-old once said to me as I passed him on the sidewalk, "But I don't want to wait until I grow up to be able to roller skate." It had looked so easy when he watched his brother and sister skate. But every time he tried, the wheels went out from under him.

We talk about babies in the nursery school—about how helpless babies are. They can't sit up. They have BMs in their pants. They have to be fed. They cannot talk. They cannot dress themselves or walk or go places. Babies need a lot of care. After a while, they get so they can walk and take care of themselves. We talk about how the nursery school children were babies once, and about how their mothers and daddies had to do everything for them. But now they can do lots of things that a baby cannot do. They can even go to school. Of course there is a danger in *over*emphasizing the helplessness of a baby, because babies do grow up and become a power to be reckoned with.

The role of each person in the family has to be discussed. The child needs to know what his daddy does at home and at work. The children enjoy books about daddies and what they do. Daddies are important in the development of children. They add something special.

> One morning Dale arrives riding on his father's shoulders. They are both radiant as if they had come on a run. Later in the morning, during play, we have this conversation:

Dale:	"We have good pickles at our house."
Mrs. S:	"Good pickles, Dale?"
Dale:	"Yes, we ate some this morning."
Mrs. S:	"For breakfast?"
Dale:	"No, we had eggs and bacon."
	(He seemed upset by my interpretation.)
	"No, my daddy and I ate them on the way to school."
Mrs. S:	"Those were extra special pickles."
Dale:	"Yes."

Daddies have a way of stretching a child's life world.

A daddy can also be puzzling to a three- or four-year-old child, especially when he starts to set limits. Most daddies are gone all day, so the young child is not as familiar with him as with the mother. Disciplining by such a father seems much more frightening to the child.

The following episode shows how a boy needed help in understanding his father's behavior.

Mr. Blake arrived with the car pool one morning.

Mr. Blake:	"Ned has something that he wants to talk over with you. He cried a long time and he wants to talk to you about it."
Mrs. S:	"All right, Ned, something that you want to talk to me about?"
Ned:	"My daddy whomped me." (He hits himself hard in the face and on his seat.) "I broke the radio."
Mrs. S:	"Your dad hit you and it didn't feel good?"
Ned:	"It hurt and I cried."
Mrs. S:	"It didn't seem right to you for your dad to hit you?"
Ned:	"No."
Mrs. S:	"Ned, you know radios are expensive. Your dad wanted to tell you as hard as he knew how not to break the radio, so you would not do it again."
Ned:	"Yes but we have two. This was the little one."
Mrs. S:	"You didn't think it mattered about the little one. But your daddy didn't want either one broken."
Ned:	"Yes."

He says this in a firm voice as he walks off. He seems to have an air of maturity as he goes into the school.

Sometimes children need help in understanding mothers when they get upset. The child needs to talk over the mother's activities. She helps take care of the house and gets meals, attends meetings, sees that everyone has clothes to wear, does what children cannot do for themselves, and has fun with everybody in the family. Some mothers choose to work outside the home or go to school, and if the child's needs are met by a good stable person, he or she may not suffer. The work the mother chooses should not be so physically or emotionally draining that it becomes difficult for her to relate to her child when at home.

The quality of the relationship between a mother and child is the important factor. Some mothers can maintain this relationship and work at the same time. The essence of parenthood is creative fidelity to the growth of the child and to the relationship. This commitment must come through to the child. Any important relationship takes a certain amount of time and cannot be established in a climate of rushing off to other activities or persons who seem to hold the real meaning of life for the parent. The child needs to feel that the mother is not indifferent to him or her, and that she participates in the details of life that are important to them.

The child should never be left with someone who does disruptive things that hurt his or her development. If the right person is found, a mother should realize that the young child may become attached to the person who meets his or her needs and may even start to call her "Mother." It is questionable if a succession of even good mother substitutes is an adequate replacement for the fundamental relationship of a mother.

A child whose mother works needs to know why, so that the child does not feel that the mother is rejecting or abandoning him or her. Some children are very sensitive about not having their mother come to school for them when they see the loving reception other children receive when their mother comes.

The work of taking care of the house and the children are part of family living, and in some ways they should be shared by husband and wife. Each family has to figure out how this work can be shared. Different families do it in different ways, according to what works best for them. Each family is different.

A good, happy relationship between husband and wife is the most crucial factor in a child's environment. A husband and wife who enjoy each other, talk together, plan together, feel that they have a life enterprise going which is theirs, have a common concern for children and an understanding of how children grow, welcome the challenge of being parents.

Feeling good about his or her family has a great deal to do with all of a child's feelings. It affects the whole Life World.

Method of Meeting Life: Life-Style

Children come to nursery school with ways of meeting life already somewhat established. Some are further along in developing healthy ways of being in the world. They have learned the fun of playing with other children, are willing to try new things, can handle a certain amount of conflict, do not depend on the teacher for ideas of what to do, can take new experiences in stride, are creative.

Other children have developed unproductive methods of being in the world such as fighting, withdrawing from relationships, taking what they want, crying, always wanting to be the center, being submissive, feeling persecuted or victimized, giving up, exploiting, and fluttering through life.

Once a method is established, it is difficult to change. The child is apt to repeat a method, whether it works or not, because it reduces anxiety, expresses anger, or is encouraged by others.

We can understand a child's method of meeting life with the help of certain questions: How does the child relate to the people and things in his world? What feeling toward life is the child acting out? Can the child explore and take risks? Can the child initiate play? How does the child solve problems and communicate with other people?

Warren is about five; he is tall and strong. Every child in the school likes him. The minute he steps into school it is as if the Pied Piper has arrived. Every child wants to say something to him or tell him what they are playing or show him something. He responds to each child who contacts him before settling down to what he wants to do or joining in something already going on.

Warren has earned this love and respect over the year. He never seems to need to protect himself (although he can), so the children feel he is safe to play with. When he enters other's play, they know he will not take away from them the chance to initiate, but will make the play more fun. He is the first one to play with a new boy who does not speak English.

One morning Sue is crying because she does not get the blue chair at juice time.

> Mrs. S: "Sue, you wanted that chair very much. You did not want Tillie to get it, but she got there first. There is another chair over there."

Warren gets up from his chair, takes Sue by the hand, and leads her to the chair next to his. He puts his arm over her shoulder while she sobs.

Warren had developed a method of meeting life that allowed him to use his creative ability, and at the same time to have warm personal relationships with his peers.

Corrine had developed a self-defeating life-style. She is a four-year-old girl whose method of meeting life is to find a safe place where she can play alone. It becomes clear that she has lost the confidence that she can form a world to live. She does not feel good about herself, and she spends a great deal of time at the table where she can play alone.

As we work with Corrine, we discover that life is coming at her too hard. Her mother and father are on the verge of divorce. Partly because her father and mother can no longer relate, she has become fragile. Things do not make sense. Her feelings are telling her to escape by withdrawing. One day she draws a picture with crayons:

> Corrine: "It's my daddy and mother on their wedding day. They're holding hands."

It is a happy picture. She is trying to put her world back together. Sensing that relationships with the other children is important in helping her rebuild her life world, we enter her play and try to enlarge it to include other children. When the other teacher is absent for two days, I ask Corrine to help the student teacher with that end of the room, "because they won't know what to do." She is very alive for two days.

When the divorce comes, she feels it deeply. One Friday she is sitting alone in the school yard. I go and sit down beside her.

Corrine:	"My daddy is coming for me today. I'm going to his house to sleep for two nights."
Mrs. S:	"So you're going to see your daddy and stay over night?"
Corrine:	"Yes, my daddy and mother don't love each other anymore, so they live with someone else."
Mrs. S:	"It is hard to have them live with someone else?"
Corrine:	"Yes."
Mrs. S:	"You still get to see both of them, even if they live with someone else?"
Corrine:	"Yes."

By helping her build successful relationships at school and by continuing to talk about her home situation, a Life World began to take shape that she could live and a new life style becomes possible. She can trust herself to go out toward people.

STRATEGY OF WORLDING   The Life World concept is a useful method of holding in mind that a person's consciousness is not mere awareness. Consciousness is intentional—at this particular moment it intends a particular style of worlded self that it is trying to bring about. For example, a world fit for discharge of tension, or a world fit for ruling others and having one's own way, or a world fit for hiding and being a safe nonentity, or a world fit for handling parents who are themselves ill-at-ease on the inside and uncertain of their connections to anything they can be true to. Or the intention can be to form a world fit for exuberant play. Any such strategy to create one's world is always a way of proclaiming "I mean."

Gradually, over a period of time, children tend to carry into many situations a picture of the *kind* of life world they want to establish. They begin to intend a style of world. No longer are they taken over by what is going on, no longer are they compliant victims of whatever strong voices they run into. They have an integrity from which they operate—a design of a mode of Life World which they believe will prevail for them in the long run. They have a world picture that is a "generalized other" (to use Mead's term), that is life-giving and life-rescuing. And so is regarded as highest and best.

COMMUNICATION   Communication is a major method of meeting life and attaching meanings to experiences. The child needs to be able to explain what he is doing, so that he does not have to attack another child physically in order to defend himself. He needs to tell people how he sees and feels about a situation so that others will take account of him. Often the most important activity going on in a child is his imagination. Other people need access to it. By talking out their imaginings play becomes more exciting and children learn to trust and enjoy each other.

Conversation is a major method by which a child puts together a world, invents enterprises, and continues to govern his development. Lifelong richness of inner world opens through hunger for communication, and through the enjoyment of being read to.

Communication has two phases—expressing and hearing. Hearing is a matter of sensing the communication within and below the words spoken, of catching what we have called "the existence condition" within the other person. Often children are already highly skilled in intuiting this level of communication. However, some do not have the words necessary to symbolize what they intuit so that they can handle it consciously. Children show remarkable growth in their ability to understand what is going on deep inside another child. They can learn to catch the complexity and the conflict, the other child's intentions, the growing he is working on, the project he is trying to bring off. They even "understand" their parents!

They also grow in their capacity to express what is on their mind in such a way that a live culture is constantly going on. The discoveries they make of themselves and life through their large color paintings are almost beyond belief—particularly when they can talk to an appreciative, respectful teacher who does not try to intrude.

The nursery school is a place where many languages of expression are experimented with and where the particular nuances of each mode are savored—the exuberance of music, the hearing of stories well told, the splashing of design in color and line, the rhythm of large muscle movements in play, the explorations and confrontations that test their utmost strength. It is a place where children are powerfully and beautifully worlding themselves. A nursery school is an incubator of communication, of communication as a style of life.

Meanings

Everything that a child does has meaning to him. Playthings are not just toys—they mean something special to each child. Each object and person in a child's world has a halo of meaning that needs to be understood by the teacher and the children playing with them.

> Adele and Andrea are three-year-old twins. Andrea is smaller than her sister and is considered by some to be less mature. Andrea is a busy little girl who does a lot of playing in the course of the morning. Although she plays on the fringes of other groups and never takes things from anybody, she seems to get what she wants.
>
> During the first two months of school, as soon as we go outside to play Andrea will run to get the only two-wheeler we have. Her legs are not long enough to reach the pedals, but she tugs and pushes until she is able to ride with ease.
>
> To Andrea the two-wheeler is big. Just sitting on it makes her feel good. She wants to break through the Life World that keeps reminding her that she is smaller and less mature than her twin. Her ability to ride the two-wheeler proves to her and to the world that she is equal to her sister. The two-wheeler is more than a plaything to Andrea. Riding it gives her the feeling of being an expanded self with an opening into life.

Sometimes a child needs help when another child tries to force a false meaning onto a situation in a way that disintegrates that child's Life World.

John's mother had died when he was only one year old, but he had been well taken care of by a father and other adults. In the bathroom one day this exchange takes place.

Terry: (In a belligerent tone, pointing her finger at John so that it touches him)
"You don't have a mother."
(John drops his head on his chest as if his whole world has collapsed.)

Mrs. S: "Yes, John had a mother. She was very kind and very pretty. She loved John very much. When he was a wee baby, she brought him to school in a buggy so I could see him. She loved him. Then she died and the real part of her went to be with God."

John: (Straightening up) "Yes."

Terry had been insinuating that there was something wrong with John because he did not have a mother. For the moment, his Life World was shattered by Terry's accusation. Something terrible was wrong with him. Perhaps he did not even deserve a mother. Helping him see her as a loving and attractive person who died from an illness helped him arrive at a positive understanding of her absence and of his own worth.

A SYSTEM OF MEANINGS   As separate meanings come to a child from experience, they are organized into a system of meanings. In the midst of ordinary play, a child may be working on the important growth of a system of meanings.

Adele is quite mature for her age. She plays easily and well with other children. For the first two months of school, she goes directly to the dolls and plays with them. She will let other children play with her and sees that they have dolls to play with. When their interest shifts to something else, she will continue to play with the dolls. Tenderly, she will wrap a doll in a blanket and sit in a rocking chair and sing.

Her world consists of mothering. She is reliving and extending the love that comes to her from her mother. This love is also becoming her way of relating to others. At first she relates to others as a mother to a child, but gradually, because of the give-and-take with other children, it becomes a relationship of love between peers. Adele is playing with dolls, but she is working on something much more fundamental. She is discovering through experience that life means working with other people as equals rather than always as a mother.

Another important part of a child's structure of meanings consists of feelings about the larger world and his relation to it. With good feelings about this world, the child can learn to handle dark moments and fears—thunder and lightning, bullies, and the death of a loved one.

School and home can help a child experience the world as something still in the process of creation, as something to which he too can contribute. When we read in nursery school about airplanes, I tell the children that a long time ago there weren't any airplanes because no one had thought of them yet. Then a man had the idea that a person ought to be able to fly if he could make wings and fasten a motor to them. I show the children what the first airplanes looked like and how people kept getting more good ideas until airplanes looked like the ones we have now. We talk about space flights and all the interesting problems that have to be solved. And perhaps they too will think up some good ideas for doing important things in the future.

A system of meanings is an important part of a child's Life World. A meaning is more than just a cognitive concept. A meaning includes feeling tones, expectations, memories of experiences, and a picture of the world. A membrane of meaning holds all of this together, giving it the definite form of an image-idea. The child symbolizes this "all-put-together world" with particular words and concepts developed in communication with other people. All experience is placed within this system and understood in terms of it.

It is extremely important that a child attach meanings to early experience that bring him or her into healthy relationships, rather than meanings that demand feeling superior to others, needing to be the center of attraction, or having to destroy others to get what is wanted. When a child's basic system of meanings is organized around seeking to understand others and constructively get along with them, that child will move toward others in a flexible and creative way.

> Tena is a small four-year-old girl from India who started school late in the spring quarter. She seems very fragile and will not play, but when she watches other children her face becomes alive. At other times her face is very serious or she looks very tired. We explain things to her and tell her that she could play with anything.
>
> One morning Tena is cautiously touching the cash register. Amy sits down beside her.
>
> > Amy: "On my first day of school, I didn't play with anything either."
>
> Amy then proceeds to explain, physically and verbally, all the things there are to do. Gesticulating, jumping up and down, she animatedly shows Tena that school is a place where you can have fun. She then starts to play with Tena and the cash register. Amy wants Tena to buy the blue telephone, but she gets no response from Tena. Quickly she switches roles so that Tena will understand how to play with her. She gives Tena the cash register and asks to buy the phone from her.
>
> > Amy: "You take the cash register, and I will buy the phone."
> >   (With a big smile, Tena understands and enters the play.)
> > Margaret: (From nearby) "Amy, come play dolls with me."
> > Amy: "We are talking about Tena now."
> >   (And she stays and plays with Tena.)

Amy was using a whole core of meanings with an intelligent flexibility. She cared for Tena. From her own experience over a year ago, she figured out how Tena was feeling and communicated this understanding to Tena. To Amy, nursery school was a place to have fun. She communicated this to Tena with all her ability and enthusiasm. When this did not work, she changed roles and became the buyer of the phone. This worked. She had brought about what she knew was possible and continued to play with Tena even when another friend tried to get her to come play dolls with her.

GROWING POWERS TO FORM MEANINGS   If children experience the important people in their lives as friendly and reliable, they begin to trust. Trust makes further sense when they discover that people are interesting to create with. Moving out toward others, being open to them, and caring for them begins to make sense and becomes important. Truth-work has begun.

Along with trust and moving out to others, reasoning about what is experienced helps develop a powerful system of meanings. Children must be able to determine the truth of what others tell them and to think through situations for themselves. Learning how to discover the truth about what we are confronting is fundamental method.

Truth-work is also the internal dialogue and decision making—the conscience work that moves the self into harmony with what is the highest and best.

Trust, thinking through, and truth-work together enable a creative and flexible system of meanings. Thus a child becomes a personal identity and a free integrity. Without these powers of forming clusters of meanings, conscience will be weak—or an enemy.

Future

Future, to the young child, means "I'm growing."

At juice time one day, after celebrating a fourth birthday, John asks each child at the table how old they are. After each child tells him, he says in a soft voice "I'm four." He says this not to boast, but as if he realizes for the first time that he is one of the older boys in the school. It puts him into a new level of being. A new future has opened up to him.

The fourth birthday is one of the most important birthdays a child will have. It is an experiential clue "I'm growing," especially if it is celebrated among peers he cares about.

After Max has his fourth birthday, he acts like a different boy. This conversation takes place with a student teacher.

Max:	"Some boy is dead in the nursery school."
Student:	(In consternation) "A boy is dead?"
Max:	"Yep, that boy named Max. The one who used to go to nursery school. He's dead."
Student:	"Oh! The three-year-old Max is dead. But now the four-year-old is alive?"
Max:	"Yep."

The future dimension of a young child's life is a glimmer "being what I am, there is something good ahead for me." As long as a child can hold onto a future, the Life World can expand and continue to reorganizing itself. When a child loses sight of the future, his Life World loses the centers of direction around which experiences are incorporated into a cohesive system of meanings. Disintegration takes place when the present does not support a future.

It is important to know what futures exist in the mind of a small child. Some are short-term futures. Many children come to school in the morning with a project in mind. One boy's hope is that he will succeed at playing with another boy who is special to him. A girl may bring a toy from home thinking that it will make her desirable to other girls. Another child may want to play with an attractive new toy to see how it works, and at the same time he is trying out being an adult. Futures have to be tried out.

Long-term futures are also being formed. A four-year-old boy who feels he is too weak to be a daddy sees no future in being one. A little girl whose feelings tell her that "my future is to be the center of an admiring group of people that I can manipulate" is developing a long-term future out of harmony with her basic need to be in relationship with peers as equals. The future of a boy who always wants to control the play is "trued-up" when another boy can say, "I don't like to play with people who never let me use my ideas."

A nursery school is full of futures being tried out. In every conflict between children, futures are at stake. A child needs help in structuring futures that are person-producing.

USEFULNESS OF THE LIFE WORLD CONCEPT FOR TEACHER AND PARENT

Organizing worlds with oneself inside is a continuing developmental task whose beginning styles and energies are formed in the first five years of life.

If we really understand the Life World concept, we can help children grow. It helps us see a child in a larger context than just one situational crisis. We need not be irritated by what he or she does. We know that a whole Life World is involved in any change, and so it is a very complex matter. Patience on our part is appropriate. Having the idea of Life World in our mind, we can better recognize the growing the child is working on. We can understand the importance of the justice culture to the formation of a person. It keeps both individual and culture in our goals.

The Life World concept has implications for planning the day at school. A child needs freedom to work on putting together his Life World. The morning has to start in a freedom-allowing way. The child soon comes to like this freedom, and starts to plan for it. He comes in the morning with the glow of expectancy on his face, an enterprise in mind, and a world he wants to live.

Play is the way a child works at building his Life World.

The child who does not have this opportunity to play suffers. Emotional stability depends on freedom to play. Feeling good about relationships is achieved in the give-and-take of play. The child's creativity is put into motion. The ability to handle problems, to initiate projects, and to carry them through is learned in self-generated play during these early years. The child who is denied this early play is apt to carry unfinished personal development into the first grade. Play is much more than learning how to initiate adult roles and activities.

This kind of freedom should not be confused with turning a child loose to hurt children or exploit equipment. Ruined equipment is of no further use to a child. The freedom we advocate allows the teacher to enter into relationship with a group of children in such a way that a culture comes into being —a nursery school culture of warmth and understanding and a justice style of living together.

The Life World concept not only affects the design of the school, it also disciplines the teacher's way of presenting a child to herself or himself. I have found that the process of writing out in detail the documented Life World of a child is a way of catching a glimpse of the living self in action. It helps me relate to the growing self of the child, and it keeps me asking, "What is he saying with his actions?" It also prevents me from ignoring the good but timid child. My attention is called to the mature child and to his need for richer experiences. I realize what the school is doing for each child. It is a potent way of learning human development and maintaining committment to the field of human development.

When I look as a teacher at the Life World of a child, the hope once more awakens that every child will become a full-functioning, spirited, loving person. Once again I search through my resources, methods, and skills to help make this existence possible.

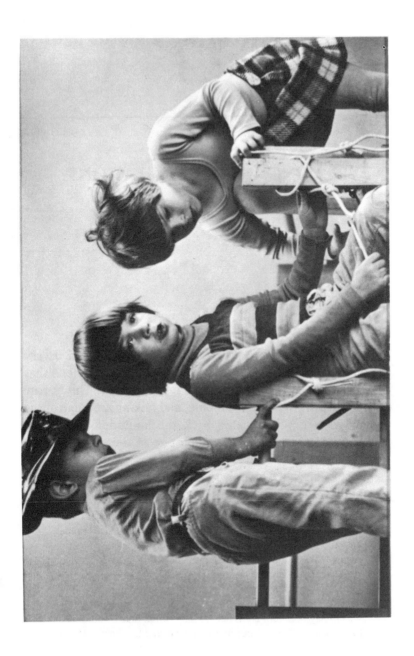

Chapter 5

BREAKING OUT OF LIMITATIONS

A person should not be a prisoner of his Life World. Every person needs the opportunity to break out of limitations that have been placed on him by others or by himself. This is true of children also. Walking, climbing, and talking are some of the regular ways a child pushes back the limitations that once confined him. The mastery of each one of these steps makes possible a whole new level of living.

Just being able to talk to others opens a world of new possibilities for a child.

Jacques was a very energetic French boy. When he started school he could not speak English. The play equipment was very stimulating to him and he entered into play with a great deal of vitality. He pushed other children out of the way. When they cried, he would get very excited and speak French. The boys started to gang up against him to protect each other. After the second day of school I was beginning to think that I would have to learn some French. But on the third day, when he was standing on top of the slide, he called, "Get out of the way. I'm coming down." The children looked at him. I smiled and nodded. They understood and got out of his way.

Jacques learned English quickly. In two weeks he was communicating. He could tell people what he wanted. The children accepted him into their play. They liked his alive creative way of life.

A new burst of power comes to the child who learns to climb and discovers that he did it and did not get annihilated.

> When Ted started school he was large for his age, and his walk was more like a waddle. Because of his energetic nature, this impediment got in his way of getting what he wanted. Bumps and falls never held him back, but just added to the frustration that built up inside him like steam.
>
> One day Ted watches the other children go up the jungle gym, walk the plank fastened to it, and then jump off the end. Ted manages to get up on the jungle gym but needs help on the plank. I hold his hand while he walks to the end and then jumps. It is solid weight that hits the ground with a thud, but his face glows with pride and he immediately goes to do it again. For two days he climbs and jumps. Eventually the waddle disappears and he can keep up with any of the boys in the school.

The nursery school teacher who believes that a child needs the opportunity to break through the limits that hold him back has a method of teaching that allows this to happen. She does not look upon learning as so many skills to be taught. Her goal is achievement supported by confidence. She provides the opportunity with all of the lures possible and allows the child the privilege of discovery, helping when needed and celebrating the achievement when it is appropriate.

There are many restrictions that freeze a child in a limited level of existence. The following are some experiences that illustrate how children can break through the limitations that hold them back.

Phony Identity

Neal is bright and physically attractive, but he cannot relate to others. Some mornings he will make a grand entrance pretending that he is Batman or some other TV character and talking in a rough, commanding way. He is secure only when he is in control and the center of the school. As Batman he will get some subservient child to be his Robin and then relate to the other children as if they were the bad guys.

One morning he is bothering the other children by telling them that they are the bad guys. Wesley is getting upset.

Mrs. S:	"Neal, did you ask Wesley if he wanted to play Batman?"
Wesley:	"I'm not a bad guy and I don't want to be."
Mrs. S:	"Wesley, you don't want to play bad guy and you don't like having Neal say that you are one. Neal, Wesley doesn't like to play bad guys."
Neal:	"But Mrs. Snyder, you can't be Batman and not have power over someone."
Mrs. S:	"If you can play Batman and not make anyone unhappy, it is all right. Otherwise you will have to think up something else to play that does not make people unhappy."

Violence had seemed right to Neal when he watched it on TV. His feelings responded to the role. Cruelty and torture became right when he was the good one getting the bad guys. The bad guys were those whom he could not control or the ones who appeared weak. The help Neal seemed to need at this point from the teacher was help in recognizing that there are limits to what he can do. And now he has reached one of them.

Neal was strong as long as he was in control. If something went wrong, his world collapsed and he fell apart. Then he tried lashing out with words, especially at adults. We worked on building up his ego strength and voicing the feelings of other children. Part of the problem was to help the children see that TV characters are not real.

One day the children are getting ready for juice time.

Wesley:	"I'm going to be the Lone Ranger when I grow up."
Neal:	"I'm going to be Superman."
Duncan:	"I'm going to be Batman."
Mrs. S:	"You know, these are not real people. They are only pretend people on TV."
Scott:	"Yes they *are* real. I saw them move."
Mrs. S:	"They can't be real or they would not be allowed to hurt people the way they do."
Duncan:	"They only hurt the bad guys."
Mrs. S:	"A real policeman is not supposed to hurt anybody, even if they are bad. He has to arrest them and take them to jail. Then a judge decides if they have done something bad. If they have, they are put in prison."
Neal:	"I'm going to be an astronaut. They are real."

By this time these characters were not so important to the children so they were able to accept this interpretation.

In the later winter, Neal took on the role of Gigantor. But this time he was a Gigantor who helped people. When the children pretended they were stranded in the snow, Gigantor went to their rescue. Later he became just Neal whom the children called for help in their play.

Neal is a leader. He moved from the need to control others by exerting power over them to finding that it was more satisfying to be a power *with* people. He found a more real leadership identity which included concern for others.

THE WORLD AS OBSTACLE

Ted is a boy who blows up with anger very fast and it blocks his rational behavior. Any person who gets in his way is an obstacle that he has to fight. Leo is a boy full of hostility. He enjoys hurting others. Ted and Leo had been fighting with each other

from the beginning of school. But the following incident occurred and brought about new roles and a caring relationship.

Ted is playing in the sandbox as I sit on the edge of the box
talking with him. Leo is riding a tricycle around the sidewalk.
He accidentally tips over going around a curve, takes a mean fall,
and starts to cry.

> Mrs. S: "Leo has hurt himself."
>   (I start to go to help him.)
> Ted: "I will help him, Mrs. Snyder."
>   (He gets there first.) "Leo, don't cry I will help
>   you."

Ted bends down and hugs him tenderly. He gets Leo on his feet,
still hugging him. Then he picks up the trike. This seems to be
very soothing to Leo. He gets on the tricycle and rides off.

It seems to me that Ted feels good about what he's done and
that any comment from me will detract from the experience. We
go back to the sandbox, but soon Leo is on the ground again near
us, pretending to cry.

> Ted: "I will help Leo."

He steps out of the sandbox and goes through the same proce-
dure. Evidently, this is very meaningful to Leo. They continue
this play; it becomes a game. Then Ted gets a trike; and he falls
off and cries. Leo takes care of him in the same way. This game
goes on for the rest of the week. Soon it becomes more than a
game between Ted and Leo; whenever a child cries Ted or Leo
are there to help.

These two boys had great potential. Each had been held
down by unresolved internal pressures that got in the way of
productive play. They had been playing together with a great
deal of friction because they were both powerful and attracted
to each other. This episode brought about a big change between
these boys. Leo was hurt and I started to help him, but Ted
heard my concern. Because he liked me, he took on my attitude.
He felt good when he helped Leo, and Leo was experiencing
Ted as some one who cared for him. They found each other as

playmates. When Ted was able to symbolize his anger, he could start to control it. Leo moved from a Life World filled with enemies that caused deep hatred and resentment into one in which he could let himself love.

TRAPPED BY MINUTE CONTROL

Gene has been weakened by having his parents do everything for him, and he resents it very much. His father usually brings him to school. Taking off Gene's snowsuit is a ritual that has to be done every day in an orderly way. Gene submits to this ritual while his father does it, but when his father sees how much faster the other children get into school, he tries to get Gene to take over the ritual. However, Gene is not allowed to take off his snowshoes the way he wants. He has to start on the left shoe first, open the strings in a certain way, spread them apart, pull the shoe open, and then take out his foot.

One morning after getting one shoe off, Gene throws the shoe to the front of his locker. This upsets the father very much.

Father: "Gene, pick up that shoe."

Gene pays no attention as he sits next to me, taking off the the other shoe. The command is repeated several times, with the same results. Finally, his father turns to me,

Father: "Gene is to pick up that shoe before he goes into school."

I nod my head, and the father leaves.

Mrs. S: "It is sort of hard to have people tell you what to do all the time, isn't it?"
Gene: "Yes."

Gene walks over, picks up his shoes, and puts them in the locker. The interesting thing is that this is the first morning that Gene is able to urinate when it is toilet time.

Gene's dilemma was his pent-up resentment over such minute control. His father is an attractive, kind, professional man. How does one break through this kind of control that comes under the guise of evident love? My recognition of Gene's inner state gave him a way out of this trap.

"THE WORLD IS TOO MUCH FOR ME"

Because he felt that the world is more than he can handle, Ivan withdrew from it. It took a long time to get him free enough to play with the toys he wanted. During the process, he goes through a period when he wants to be very close to the adults of the school. He will come up to us from behind and cling to our shoulders. We squeeze him tight and put him down in the midst of play. One of the student teachers helps him a great deal one morning:

Ivan is building with blocks on the floor and the student is sitting near him. Ivan comes over and crawls up on the student's shoulders. The student leaves him there for a while, then says to him, "When you can be close to someone, you feel more loved?" The student squeezes him hard and puts him down.

After this Ivan seems to be able to play on his own with other children. He likes to wrestle when we are outside, and we try to reinforce his strong feelings. Ivan begins to feel new strength and warmth. One day he looks out the window.

Ivan: "See, there is a monster out there, Mrs. Snyder."

I am disappointed to hear this because we had thought his fears had disappeared.

Mrs. S: "A monster out there, Ivan?"
Ivan: "A monster and his head is off."
Mrs. S: "A monster without a head?"
Ivan: "A not very good monster without his head."
Mrs. S: "A monster can't be much of a monster without his head?"
Ivan: "No, I got him."

Mrs. S:	"You got that old monster out there?"
Ivan:	"Yes."
	(With real strength)

The breakthrough is beginning for Ivan. He is a gifted boy with a great deal of creative ability, but it had become paralyzed in a body filled with fear. His energies did not dare come out. He has moved from withdrawal to taking charge of his world.

REACHING INTO EXUBERANCE

Sometimes a teacher's lack of perception can prevent a child from breaking through limitations.

When she started school, Linda was a very proper little girl with a great deal of ability. She liked nursery school and was enjoying her new freedom and fun. Then she went on a two-week vacation in November.

On the day she comes back it is raining, so we have to stay inside all morning. We get out the Tinker Toys near the end of the morning. This is the first time we have used them. Leo, Dean, Margery, Gerry, and Jay are building at the end of the room, where I am. They are making an elaborate and fragile lollipop machine. I am glad this group of children is having a good experience playing together, and I want it to succeed. Linda comes up in back of me, grabs me around the neck, and tries to spill me.

Mrs. S: "Linda, you want to play, but I am busy."

Linda goes to the other end of the room and does the same thing to a student teacher, but the student does not understand her either. Linda comes back to our area and grabs part of the lollipop factory.

Mrs. S: "Linda, that is part of the factory we are building. See, we are making lollipops. Give it to me, please?"

She throws it and grabs another piece. I pick her up and put her on the block cupboard next to us.

Mrs. S: "Linda, I can't let you break our factory."
Linda: (A few moments later) "I won't break it any more."
Mrs. S: "All right, you may get down then."

This little girl was trying to free herself from being such a proper little girl. My preoccupation with the others and lack of perception threw a block in Linda's way. It would have helped if I had perceived her as a little girl who had played this way in the school yard before she was absent and was now trying to re-establish physical contact in play relationship as she had remembered it. She wanted the intimacy she remembered from before. She was saying, "See, I am here."

Breaking the lollipop machine was not her intention. She was contacting me vigorously, not cautiously as she had done before. This was a new dimension in her life. A good reply to her at the beginning of the episode would have been, "It would be fun to wrestle like we did outside before you went to visit your grandmother. I'm glad you are back again. Right now I'm building this lollipop machine with these people." This would have given her a clue that I understood and valued her. Probably the rest of the incident would not have happened. She would not have needed to break the lollipop machine to make me see her. A teacher's lack of perception can get in the way of a child who is trying to find a new level of living.

COMPULSIVE DRIVE TO ORGANIZE A LIFE WORLD

Sometimes overwhelming events happen to a child and cause a secure life world to become fragile.

Trudy's Life World falls apart when her family has to live in a motel for four months while their new house is being finished.

I can understand what she is doing when she gathers up all the play dough each morning and does not want others to play with it. She is struggling to establish her Life World once more.

I make larger amounts of play dough so there will be plenty for everyone, but she wants all of it. It is difficult to be understanding and at the same time to prevent her from solving problems in the wrong way.

> Mrs. S: "Trudy, it feels good to have all the play dough. You may have it all until someone wants some."

But when another child asks for some, she will not share it.

> Mrs. S: "Trudy, it feels so good to play with all the play dough! John, you want some play dough too, so you can make things?"

It is still too difficult for her to share it.

> Mrs. S: "Trudy, you like having it all very much. But I'm going to take some now so John can play too."

This she accepts.

Two significant episodes happen as Trudy is working through her difficulty.

One Monday morning in January many of the children have arrived and are taking off their coats in the locker room. The children in the car pool arrive with much excitment. Trudy comes in bringing a new pink set of housekeeping equipment—vacuum cleaner, broom, dust pan, and dust mop.

> Trudy: "These are mine and I'm not going to let anyone use them."
> Mrs. S: "O Trudy, new and pink. And you got them for your birthday."
> Trudy: "Yes, and I'm not going to let anyone use them."

By this time all of the children were trying to get them. I was sitting on the bench, so I pick up Trudy with the toys and put her on my lap.

Lee:	"Mrs. Snyder, I don't know what to do about girls."
Mrs. S:	"You don't know how to get things you want from girls, Lee?"
Lee:	"No."
Mrs. S:	"Trudy is afraid that you will break her new playthings. She got them for her birthday."
Lee:	"I won't break them, Trudy."
Bob:	"I won't break them."
	(The girls say the same thing and start to take them.)
Trudy:	"They can't have them."
Mrs. S:	"Trudy is having a hard time thinking about letting anybody play with her things. Wait a minute."
Trudy:	"I won't let them have them. They are only for me to play with."
Mrs. S:	"Trudy, if you bring them inside, you need to share them. If you don't want to share them, then you may leave them in your locker."
	(The children start to take them again.)
Mrs. S:	"Just a minute. Trudy has not decided whether she is going to take them inside."
Trudy:	"I will let the girls play with them, but not the boys."
Mrs. S:	"You feel that the girls will take good care of them but not the boys."
Trudy:	"Yes, but not the boys."
Mrs. S:	"The boys said they would take good care of them too, and if they don't, we will not let them play with them."
	(She thinks a little longer.)
	"Why don't you choose the one you want to play with and let the others take turns with the rest."
Trudy:	"I will play with this."

She keeps the vacuum cleaner and hands me the other things. I give the children short turns with them and they are very careful. After a while, Trudy trades the vacuum cleaner for the broom and dustpan so all of the children have turns with it also. After the children seem satisfied, I gather up her housekeeping set.

Mrs. S: "Trudy, everybody enjoyed playing with your housekeeping set very much. Do you want me to put it in your locker now?"

Trudy: "Yes."

This was a real sharing experience for Trudy, not the phony forced sharing that occurs when a teacher or parent makes a child share against her will. Here, Trudy could have refused to share without feeling guilty and could have put her toys in her locker for safe keeping.

The initial barrier to sharing was her fear that her toys might be damaged. Once we took this fear seriously and helped her see that both teacher and the other children would see that they were protected, she was able to share them.

If she had continued then to insist that only certain special friends or girls could play with them, she would clearly have been trying to use the toys to manipulate and possibly hurt other children, to buy friends and to hurt those she excluded. When a toy is so used, it is no longer a tool for growth shared by all. It has become a symbol of power and a way of controlling others. Those not permitted to play are forced to deal with feelings of rejection, jealousy, and anger. Conflict, mistrust, rivalries, and aggression ensue. This creates a climate in which learning to share becomes impossible.

If a teacher agrees to the prejudicial use of toys, the caring atmosphere of the school is destroyed. The teacher, who allows a child to do whatever he or she wishes, is in reality saying, "I do not care about the feelings of those who are excluded." In this situation, I think that I managed to say, "I care for you, your property, and for everybody in the school. I will work to help us find a way to share your toys safely, and to benefit from their use." When such a venture works, it becomes the basis of a sharing life-style. Trudy also picked up some fears while living in the motel. They became symbolized by ghosts.

> One morning, Trudy is painting at the easel. She tells me that she is going to paint all over the paper, and that she is going to paint a long time. After a while she tells me she is done and asks me to put her name on it. The picture had a small yellow object in the middle with heavy blue all around it. I start to put her name on it in yellow paint over the blue at the top.

> Trudy: "I want my name in blue, Mrs. Snyder."
> Mrs. S: "I didn't think that blue would show on the blue, Trudy."
> Trudy: "Make it blue. I want blue."
> Mrs. S: "All right. But I am not sure that it will show." (I print her name in blue.) "It does show, Trudy."
> Trudy: (Pointing to the yellow part.) "This is a ghost."
> Mrs. S: The yellow part is a ghost?"
> Trudy: "Yes, an old scary ghost."
> Mrs. S: "And the blue part?"
> Trudy: "The blue part is doing away with the ghost."
> Mrs. S: "Getting the best of that old scary ghost."
> Trudy: "Yes, knocking down the ghost."
> Mrs. S: "You don't want that old scary ghost bothering you anymore, so you are knocking him down."
> Trudy: "Yes."

> She put her finger in the blue of the picture and streaked the blue over the ghost with strong motions.

After I understood her picture, it was evident why she wanted her name in blue. These two episodes happened during the same week. After this, life seemed easier for Trudy. The houses that she built in the housekeeping corner, using chairs for walls, became bigger and she could allow more children into them.

Inner Panic

When Sonia started school at three-and-a-half years of age, she was physically well developed. Her doctor wants her to wear special shoes both day and night to correct her arches. Her speech is slurred at first, and she makes up words when she does not have words to get the relationship she wants. On the first day of school, to my surprise, she lets out a terrific noise whenever something happens that she does not like. She continually calls to me in a demanding tone.

On the second day of school I discover that she will not step on the grass. She is on the sidewalk and I am on the grass.

Sonia:	"Mrs. Snyder."
Mrs. S:	"You want something, Sonia?"
Sonia:	(In a demanding way) "Yes, come here."
Mrs. S:	"Come over here, Sonia."
Sonia:	"No, you come over here."
	(She seems to be afraid even of the idea of getting on the grass.)
Mrs. S:	"Sonia, it is all right for you to step on this grass. The grass is to play on here at school. You may step on it."
Sonia:	"No."
Mrs. S:	"There is something about the grass that you don't like?"
Sonia:	"Yes."

She stomps one foot on the grass as if to kill something. I repeat the same gesture with my right foot. She does it again and so do I. Then I try it with my left foot. She does the same. Then I jump on the grass with two feet, but she turns and leaves. I realize that I am trying too hard to get her on the grass, and I will have to wait until she is ready to do it herself.

The next day Sonia is very alive. She is busy from the time that she walks in. Her speech is more direct and her walk is also. Outside she stays on the sidewalk calling for me, "Come here." I go as often as I can.

A few days later she is playing with a student teacher in the school yard.

Sonia:	"Go to the store."
	(She points to the window of the house next door across the grass.)
ST:	"You want me to go to the store? Do you want to go to the store with me?"
Sonia:	"No, you go alone."
Winston:	"I'll go to the store with you, Sonia."
Sonia:	"No."

After this incident the staff decides not to try to get her to go on the grass until she offers to make the move herself. The fear is deeper than we first thought.

We wait almost a month for her to get ready. Then one day she goes to a student teacher and takes her hand. The student had played with her on the days when she was in school.

Sonia:	"I want to go to bed."
ST:	"Where, Sonia?"
	(Sonia starts across the grass toward the trailer, but she stops in the middle of the yard. It seems that she realized all of a sudden that she is on the grass.)
ST:	"You want to take me to the trailer to go to bed?"
	(Sonia starts again. When they get there she wants to walk up the ramp.)
ST:	"Your shoes are the slippery kind, Sonia. I will help you."
Sonia:	"Now lie down."

They play and Sonia is very happy. Later that day her mother comes for her and lifts her down from the trailer, and they walk across the grass together.

On the next day she does not go on the grass and we do not try to get her to do so. On the following day she takes my hand and takes me to the trailer, but it takes two more weeks before she is free to go on the grass by herself.

One day she is running and having fun on the sidewalk with Mrs. Alexander, the other teacher, and some of the children. They are throwing leaves at each other. Sonia is radiantly happy. Near the end of the morning Mrs. Alexander and I are standing on the grass talking. Sonia comes and joins us.

Sonia:	"Mrs. Snyder, I am on the grass."
Mrs. S:	"Sonia, you are on the grass. Mrs. Alexander is on the grass. I am on the grass."
Sonia:	(In a very loud voice, stamping her foot) "Pow!"
Mrs. S:	"Pow!"
Sonia:	(Louder) "Pow!"
Mrs. S:	(Trying to match her intensity) "Pow!"
Sonia:	(She holds her hands up high. Her whole body shakes.) "Pow!"
Mrs. S:	(As loud as I can say it) "Pow!"
Sonia:	(She shakes and twists.) "Pow!!!"

We stand for a while, then I leave to put away the tricycles.

Sonia: "Mrs. Snyder, come back on the grass."

After this, Sonia moved freely on the grass. In three months she had shattered not just one limit, but several. Her's was a dramatic story. We were careful not to work directly on her panic about grass. We knew that the healing of the whole child was necessary and that she would handle this herself when she felt ready, and the needed relationship was available. She has a great deal of ability and drive. Her world will have to be a big one to use all the energy that is stored in her one body.

FREEDOM FROM ANGER

Sometimes it takes a long time for a child to come through. Grant was a very interesting boy and we are going to follow him through a series of episodes.

Grant enters school in December. He is a physically well developed and attractive four-and-a-half year old. When I visited him in his home before he started school, he did not talk much. A very energetic younger brother kept coming between us when I tried to tell Grant about our school. Both his father and mother said that Grant was shy.

During the first two weeks of school, Grant does very little playing. He sits beside me or follows me around the school. I notice that he is watching the other children a great deal.

Gradually he starts to play, but he will pretend that he is a fierce animal—a lion, tiger, or bear—using his hands like claws to go after the faces of the children. This disrupts their play.

One day Jay, Gloria, Bess, and Jerry are playing family in the housekeeping corner. I hear Jay tell Grant to go away because Grant is bothering them. Then Jay calls to me.

Jay: "Mrs. Snyder, Grant is bothering us."
        (I go to help them.)
Mrs. S: "Jay, you people were playing house and having fun. Grant, you want to play too. But when you play like a tiger and start clawing, it messes up their play."

Grant withdraws from the group and stands around watching. Pretty soon he is bothering some other children. He follows this pattern most of the time, not hitting but clawing close to the face.

Russ, Dick, and Steve are busy playing firemen on top of the jungle house. Grant enters the play.

Steve: "We don't want you up here."
Mrs. S: "Steve, you were having fun being firemen and don't like the way Grant is playing? But the jungle house is for everybody."
Grant: "I'm a tiger fireman."
Mrs. S: "Grant, you want to be a fireman, but a fierce animal fireman spoils the play."
        (He leaves the play.)

About this same time he starts to follow children and grab them from the back.

Mrs. S: "Grant, you would like to play with Jay, but he doesn't like it when you grab him like that."

Nonetheless, Grant continues to grab like this from time to time.

One morning Grant finds the doll family on top of the green box where others had left it. He starts to play with the dolls. First he has the father and mother kiss each other.

Mrs. S: "They like each other."
Grant: "Yes."

Then he puts the baby in the mother's arms.

Mrs. S: "The mother is holding the baby?"

He stands up on the box and the mother throws the baby all the way down to the floor.

Mrs. S: "The mother must not like the baby to hurt it so."

We are interrupted, so I cannot help him further.

The animal play with other children goes on for weeks. When I enter the play he stops playing and withdraws from all play for a while. He keeps changing the animals he imitates.

The pictures that he draws at the table are interesting and puzzling. He especially likes to draw on the days we have out crayons or markers. He tells Mrs. Huffman, the other teacher, about one.

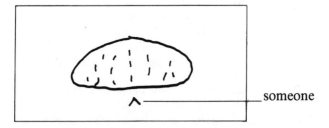

Mrs. H: "That is an interesting picture, Grant."
Grant: "It's the rising sun over grass as someone watches."

We interpret this to mean he is outside the exciting world of nursery school looking on. Then he starts a series of animal pictures that continue for two months.

Grant:	"This is a river."
	(straight lines in middle)
ST:	"A river, Grant?"
Grant:	"And here's a snake."
	(Wiggly line on left side)
ST:	"A snake?"
Grant:	"And here's a boy."
	(curved line on right side)
ST:	"The boy is on the other side of the water from the snake?"
Grant:	"Yes, the snake can't get the boy across the water."
ST:	"Can't get the boy."
Grant:	"But the boy has to go across the water to get the snake."
	(He draws footsteps across the water.)
ST:	"Now the boy is across the water by the snake."
Grant:	"And here comes a big bear!"
	(Footprints on top of page)
ST:	"Oh, there's a bear?"
Grant:	"Yes, he's going to eat the two boys."
	(He calls the boy and snake two boys.)
ST:	"The bear is after the boys?"
Grant:	"Yes, here is a net to snag the bear. It will catch him."
	(He uses pink and draws over the bear.)
ST:	"The pink net will catch the bear?"
Grant:	"Yes, it will go all over him and he can't get out."
	(Then he draws a big X over the whole picture.)
	"Put my name on it."

On February 4 he draws another picture. Mrs. Huffman is sitting close by.

	Grant:	"This is a snake."
		(Curved line in middle)
	Mrs. H:	"A snake, Grant?"
	Grant:	"He has two things in his mouth."
	Mrs. H:	"Two things?"
	Grant:	"Yes, here's the sun."
		(The mark in the upper right)
		"It's going to melt it all away."
	Mrs. H:	"The sun is going to melt it all away?"
	Grant:	"Yes, but here's a bird."
		(The mark in the upper left.)
		"It's going to fly to the sun."
	Mrs. H:	"Oh, the bird will fly away to the sun?"
	Grant:	"Then there's a big noise."
		(He draws a large circle around the picture.)
		"They don't know what it is. But it's a big bear."
	Mrs. H:	"A big bear, Grant?"
	Grant:	"And here is the bear's mouth."
		(Red mouth.)
		"He's smiling."
	Mrs. H:	"Oh, the bear is smiling?"
	Grant:	"Yes, when he smiles his teeth show."
	Mrs. H:	"The bear has teeth?"
	Grant:	"Yes, and he's going to eat them."

He hands Mrs. Huffman the crayon and tells her to put his name on it.

We think Grant does not know how to play with toys, so we take every opportunity to play with him. But he does not seem interested. We do not seem to be making progress with helping him. Mondays are especially difficult.

One Monday as I watch him I realize that he seems to be enjoying breaking up others' play. The fierce animals are a guise to do what he wants to do. I had been misunderstanding him when I said, "You want to play." He wants to hurt back the world. The animals are his way of getting sanctions for doing things he does not dare do as Grant.

He is especially disruptive to the family play. Evidently, since he cannot find a satisfactory role in his own family, he cannot allow himself to take a role in the children's family play. He is trying to break it up. So I decide to name what he was trying to do.

Jay:	"Mrs. Snyder, Grant won't stop."
Mrs. S:	"Grant, I believe you are trying to break up their play. Sometimes you wish you could be a lion and claw and hurt people?"
Grant:	"Yes."

That morning Dexter had brought Oscar, a hand puppet, to school. The children like it very much and it is passed from child to child. Finally Grant gets it and immediately starts to use it in an aggressive way toward other children.

Grant:	(Snapping at their faces) "I'm a cookie monster."
Mrs. S:	"Grant, if you want to play mean, I will play with you."
	(We go to a corner where we can be alone. I encouraged his rough play of snapping at my face.)
	"Boy, you are a rough Oscar."
	"Wow!"
	(After a while.)
	"I'll have to figure out what to do about such a rough Oscar."
	(He drops the puppet on the floor and walks away.)
Grant:	"I'm done, Mrs. Snyder."

For the rest of that week and for another week he seems to get along better. I begin to think that he had made it.

Around this time he makes another interesting picture.

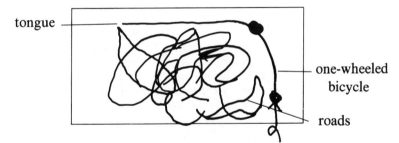

tongue

one-wheeled bicycle

roads

Grant:	"These are roads."
	(Curved and overlapping lines of various colors.)
	"They're all mixed up roads."
	(He makes a vertical line down the right side of the paper with a circle at bottom and a bump at top.)
	"It's a one-wheeled bicycle."
Mrs. H:	"A tall one-wheeled bicycle?"
Grant:	"Yes, a one-wheeled bicycle."
Mrs. H:	"Someone is riding the one-wheeled bicycle?"
Grant:	"Yeah. Here's his tongue."
	(Horizontal line all the way across the top.)
	"He's sticking it out."
Mrs. H:	"The man is riding the one-wheeled bicycle and he is sticking his tongue out?"
Grant:	"Yeah, he's sticking his tongue out."
	(He adds some red to the middle part.)
	"Here's a road and he drives on it. Brr, brr!"
Mrs. H:	"And this brown part?"
Grant:	"It's roads too. Black, brown, all roads. Green too."
Mrs. H:	"And the yellow?"
Grant:	"Yeah."
	(He gives her a crayon and tells her to put his name on it.)

On the following Monday he comes in announcing that he is Spiderman. He uses his hands like claws to spread webs over other children as they play. This too was disruptive.

Mrs. S:	(Hoping to enable him to play) "Grant, you like being Spiderman, but can you be a Spiderman that plays so it will be fun for everybody?"

This seems to be more than he can do.

> Mrs. S: "Grant, when you play Spiderman it just causes us too much trouble. Wait until we go outside to be Spiderman."
> (The children had been playing Superman and other TV characters outside. I thought he could fit into this play.)

To my surprise he accepts this suggestion, then forgets to ask to be Spiderman outside.

Inside on the next day, he is not as aggressive. Jay and Myles are building a city using wooden blocks. They are talking a lot while doing it. Grant edges in and puts his hands on some of the blocks.

> Jay: "Grant, get out!"
> Mrs. S: "Jay, that is such a nice city you have. Grant, you like Jay's city and you would like to build a skyscraper too?"
> Jay: "He can have these. But he is not to touch these. He can build there."
> Mrs. S: "It's all right for Grant to use these for his skyscraper, but you don't want him to bother your buildings?"

They play together for a while. Then Jay and Myles leave to play something else. In a short time Grant knocks down the whole city.

> Mrs. S: "Grant, Jay and Myles left, and now it is fun to knock it all down."
> Grant: "Yes."

On February 25 he draws another interesting picture. Mrs. Huffman is sitting at the table also drawing.

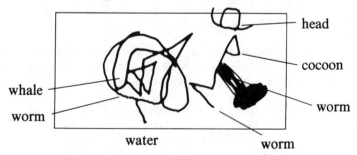

Grant: "Look at mine."

Mrs. H: "Yes, Grant you are making a picture too."

Grant: "It's water."

(Lines at the bottom left)

Mrs. H: "Oh, water?"

Grant: "And a whale."

(Triangle on left)

Mrs. H: "A whale?"

Grant: "Yes, he lives in the water. And a worm. (Diagonal lines at right) He lives in the water too. He's going to eat the whale."

Mrs. H: "Oh, the worm is going to eat the whale?"

Grant: "Yes, he's going to eat him all up. And another worm. (Diagonal lines in center) He's just jumping."

Mrs. H: "He's not eating the whale?"

Grant: "No, he's just jumping. And he jumps up in a cocoon. And he'll come out and be a butterfly and fly all around. He needs wings."

Mrs. H: "You're going to make the butterfly some wings?"

(He pulls the picture back and draws another part.)

Mrs. H: "You made some wings for the butterfly?"

Grant: "No, it's his head."

(Circle in upper right)

Mrs. H: "Oh, his head."

Grant: "He's poking it out and he sees all the people." (He looks around the school.)

Mrs. H: "He sees the people in the nursery school."

Grant: "And he hears them."

Mrs. H: "He knows the people too."

Grant: "He hears them and he says what they say."

Mrs. H: "The butterfly says the same things the people say."

Grant: "Then he pulls his head inside."

Mrs. H: "He pulls his head back inside, but someday he'll come out of the cocoon and then he can fly."

Grant: "Yes. Put my name on it."

(Mrs. Huffman puts his name on it. He also asks her to put his last name on it.)

The picture makes us think that Grant is about ready to make it. Then one day after rest period, Grant comes into the room and starts putting on his coat.

> Grant: "I'm going to be Spiderman outside."
>   (I am disappointed to hear this.)
>   "I'm going to be Spiderman."
> Mrs. S: "There is something about Spiderman you like?"
> Grant: "Yes, he hurts people."
> Mrs. S: "Sometimes, you would like to hurt people?"
> Grant: "Yes, like Spiderman."
> Mrs. S: "When you feel mean on the inside, you would like to hurt people?"
> Grant: "No! When I feel mean on the *outside*."
>   (He holds up his claws. I feel that he has a new softness in his face and body.)

With this Grant goes out the door into the yard. I decide to follow him and see if I can help him be a Spiderman that children can tolerate. Jay, Tilly, Dick, and Bess are playing Superman, each child becoming a different character. They are pushing each other in a vigorous but playful way. Grant joins the play, but he gets too pushy with Dick.

> Mrs. S: "Dick, tell Grant to stop when he gets too rough. And you will stop, won't you Grant, when he tells you?"

He does stop when they tell him. I stay close to say it whenever he gets too rough. All of them are enjoying the game. After about five minutes of good play, Bess pushes Grant too hard and knocks him down. I go to him. He clings hard to me around the legs. I get down and hug him.

> Mrs. S: "They got too rough, Grant?"
>   (He starts to cry, big tears roll down his cheeks. This is the first time I have seen him cry. I hug him tight. He sobs very hard, as if it is coming from deep inside him. He puts his head on my shoulder and seems to rest on it in a heavy way.)
>   "They wouldn't stop and you couldn't say 'stop'?"

Grant:	"I said stop."
Mrs. S:	"When people get too rough it hurts a lot, doesn't it, Grant?"
Grant:	"I said 'stop' but they wouldn't stop." (His sobbing is easing.)
Mrs. S:	"Grant, when you tell them to stop, you have to say it very loud so they are sure to hear you."

Before in his anger, there was no one he felt he could tell his pain or anger to. In his sobbing he opens himself to me and finds there is a world that cares for him. He is able to let go of his old world and has some feeling that he can live in the new world.

This seems to mark the end of Grant's angry self. It has taken five long months of agonizing experiences to help Grant like himself, to want to be in relationship, and to begin to care for the children in the school.

One day the children are in the bathroom at toilet time.

Russ:	(Puting his head close to Grant's) "Grant has a new face."
Mrs. S:	"Yes, now Grant knows how to play and have fun." (Grant is pleased.)
Tilly:	"I like him now."
Bess:	"We all like him now."

We wished that the year could have been longer so that his new identity could have had a longer chance to get established.

LIVING SPACE FOR CHILDREN

Breaking out of limitations is an important part of our theory. The limitations we are concerned with are those that prevent a child from being in relationship. Of course all nursery schools need limits. A child should not be allowed to hurt another child or break equipment. In this chapter we are talking mainly about internal limitations that prevent a child from developing a healthy Life World.

Many children of nursery school age need help and a warm environment to free themselves from restrictions that prevent them from functioning fully. Nursery school is the step between the home and the task-centered school. It is not an extension of the home; it is the children's world. Each child ought to be free to organize a world from the new possibilities that are there, so that he or she can walk into the world ahead with big strides.

Part II

FUNCTIONS OF THE TEACHER AS
SIGNIFICANT ADULT

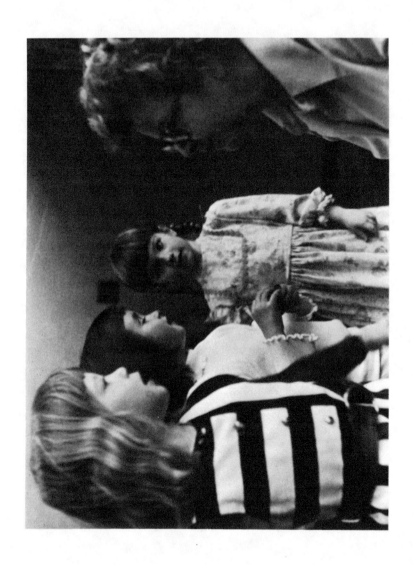

Chapter 6

ENABLING THROUGH THE UNDERSTANDING MODE OF CONVERSATION

Understanding is more than listening; it includes valuing, excellence of expression, and two-way communication. Understanding is not just a "method" to be used as a gimmick or to conduct "therapy." Understanding is a means of developing humanness.

In the midst of all the play and aliveness in the nursery school, the teacher spends a great deal of time explaining things. But the best way to help a child with his or her personal growth is by understanding.

Understanding communicates to the child that "I care for you; what you say and feel is important." Understanding is hearing not only the words of a child, but also hearing the struggling, growing self. It is hearing the whole of the child and not just the emotional outbreak. The teacher stands with the child in his life situation until the child feels that the teacher is in relationship with him as he is. The child comes to feel that he is known even as he knows himself. At the same time he senses that he will not be rejected, that the teacher will stay in relationship with him.

The goal of understanding is more than relationship. The goal is to empower the child to understand himself and do it on his own. As he learns to comprehend himself, he becomes experienced in understanding others.

Understanding is good for all children—the timid child, the regressed child, the tense child, the child filled with hostility, the healthy child.

We use four forms of understanding in the school:

1. Understanding verbal content
2. Hearing and helping child clarify feelings
3. Understanding the child's existence situation
4. Reconstructing an episode with feelings and intentions

A nursery school teacher needs to be so skilled in all four of these forms that they become spontaneous.

UNDERSTANDING VERBAL CONTENT

A child comes alive when you respond in such a way as to let him know you understand what he has said. The secret of this kind of conversation with a child is to listen in such a way that you catch the most important thing to him in his communication. This might be thought of as locating his peak of significance, from which further conversation will come. You put this into fresh language to give him a fuller grasp of it. The child feels, "Yes, the teacher got what I meant," and he continues developing his story. He leads the conversation, creating as he talks.

Here is a conversation with a three-year-old boy one morning in the coat room.

> Ron: "Guess what, Mrs. Snyder! We got kittens."
> Mrs. S: "Kittens, Ron?"
>   (With enthusiasm)

Ron: "Kittens! And they were born on my bed."

Mrs. S: "Kittens born on your bed!"

Ron: "My mother was just ready to put the mother cat out so I could go to bed, when one of the kittens was coming out."

Mrs. S: "So the mother cat had her kittens on your bed!"

Ron: "Yes, the mother cat had her kittens on my bed, and I had to sleep on another bed!"

Mrs. S: "You gave up your bed for the cats?"

Ron: "You know what? The mother cat picks up the kittens with her teeth by the fur."

Mrs. S: "The mother cat can carry the kittens with her teeth!"

Ron: "Yes, and now she put them in my mother's closet."

I was helping a three-year-old boy tell his story. It was his story, so I did not take it away from him. I could have told him all I know about cats, but that would have taken away his delight. I was entering into his enthusiasm and intensity about the cats. I was participating in the spirit of the occasion, and this was communicated by my words and tone of voice. I was not parroting what he said, I was participating in his delight as well as listening to his story. Because I understood him, he kept telling me about his cats for the rest of the year. Even as you understand the verbal content, more than words are understood. You concentrate on the child's words so that he can tell you his story.

Again, understanding is not parroting back what a child has said. Parroting is repeating words without entering into the child's thinking and feeling. It does not communicate the teacher's aliveness. Catching the essence of what the child is saying and putting it into fresh words takes real concentration. The important point is to respond to what the child has said and not to jump ahead.

Sometimes it is difficult to put what a child is saying into your own words because the statements are so short. To keep the child talking, the teacher can use the child's key words, but not necessarily the complete sentences. Sometimes incomplete sentences are enough to help the child extend her thoughts.

Only when the teacher is completely confused about the child's meaning is an exact repetition of his words appropriate. In such a situation, to prevent distortion or misinterpretation the teacher should stick to the child's words, hoping the child will try again. What the child is feeling and doing has to be symbolized, and this can best be done by using some fresh words which show that you too are thinking.

Understanding does not mean that at other times the teacher cannot express her own ideas and feelings. To carry on ordinary conversation two people need to reveal their own feelings as well as help each other develop their story.

Verbal content understanding is only the first step toward understanding.

HEARING AND HELPING A CHILD CLARIFY FEELINGS

Strong feelings are important. They are the driving force that helps a person become fully functioning. Everyone has a right to his or her feelings. The expression of feelings is necessary to prevent them from being repressed and becoming destructive. The value of expressing feelings is to get them up where they can be processed in such a way that all of the person stays in control of the growing. Only processed feelings enlarge consciousness.

Deeper Than Verbal Content

Hearing and helping a child clarify his feelings is a deeper level of understanding than catching the verbal content. Sometimes a child's words do not communicate the true feelings beneath them.

On the second day of school, Adeline is longingly watching the boys playing on top of the green box and going down the slide.

Adeline:	"I don't like boys."
	(She seems very interested in what they are doing.)
Mrs. S:	"You would like to play with them?"
Adeline:	"Yes, but I don't know how."

So I showed her how to climb up on the box and explained to her how to take turns. She played with the boys on the slide for the rest of the period, and a very proper, inhibited little girl moved toward becoming an adventuresome self.

In Adeline's case, her words hid her real feelings. How off-base the teacher would have been if she had responded literally to Adeline's words and taken the real issue to be her hatred of masculinity. She would have been leading Adeline down some strange canyon that had nothing to do with her real situation. Adeline needed help to put words to her feelings. I was trying to catch the feelings that were forming the words. She was hesitatingly wanting to try out a new level of living. When the right words were provided for her to understand this, she was able to act in a way that greatly enlarged her Life World. She became a spirited self that could relate to energetic boys, taking on a big world that had previously contained impossible obstacles.

This understanding is not merely a technique or the use of the right words. It is a mode of relationship. It cannot be used as a subtle means of manipulating the child. And it needs to be a response to the child's immediate feelings, not to what the adult remembers the child felt at some other time.

Processing—Not Just Expressing

Recently a great deal of emphasis has been placed on helping children express their feelings. The expression of feelings is important because it prevents feelings from getting bottled up inside a person, where they fester. However, it is becoming clear that it matters how this expression is done and for what goal it is pursued. Expressing feelings is just the first step in a longer process of reconstructing a positive relationship with others.

A statement of a feeling such as "ouch, you hurt me," or "I want that" is often destructively combined with name calling to destroy another's self-esteem or with an aggressive attack to cause pain. Children need to learn to communicate their feelings effectively without also degrading or hurting the other person. Expressing negative feelings to control others or to build up an inaccurate sense of persecution imprisons the self and creates a self-deceptive inner speech. Expression of feelings as a first step in a process moving toward restoring a constructive positive relationship is self-liberating and self-actualizing.

Children's feelings and desires are very complex and occur within a larger context. Any one request is often made in the context of more important but unstated requests. Feeling contains a long-term valuing component and a strategy for building a Life World. If you only catch the emotional outburst you are not recognizing the total feeling. The self, struggling to carry out the feeling "I want it," needs help to stay in positive relationship with others and not to lose their friendship. Within all feeling is a yearning for productive relationship. In expressing feelings a child is not merely discharging pent-up emotion, but striving for meaningful relationship.

> On the first day of school, Pat sees Roy playing with a small fire engine. Roy is busy fastening the hose to the engine, putting out fires, parking the engine in an imaginary fire station. Pat watches for few seconds then grabs the fire engine. Roy tries to pull it away from Pat, but Pat holds tight and starts kicking Roy. The scuffle develops into a real fight, with both boys crying and pulling.

> Mrs. S: (Getting down to put an arm around each so we can talk) "Wait up."
> Roy: (Still grabbing for it) "It's mine."
> Pat: (Pulling it farther out of Roy's reach) "I want it."

Roy: "He took it."

Pat: "It's mine."

Mrs. S: "Roy, you were playing with the fire engine and Pat took it away from you?"

(I am trying to get back to the situation from which the feelings came. Pat still struggles to get away.)

"Pat, you like the fire engine very much. You want to play with it too?"

(I take the fire engine. Pat still does not want to give it up, but he stops struggling.)

Pat: "But I want it."

Mrs. S: "Pat, you do want it. So, Roy, finish your turn. Pat, then you can play with the fire engine."

(I give it to Roy. Pat starts to cry again.)

"Roy, I will tell you when your turn is done."

(Pat continues to cry. It is more like a whine.)

"Pat, it is hard to wait for your turn, isn't it?"

(Pat stops crying.)

"Pat, you want to fasten the hose onto the fire engine and squirt out the fire?"

Pat: "Yes, I want it now."

Mrs. S: "Pat, you want the fire engine very much, but Roy likes the fire engine very much also. It is going to be hard for him to give it up when I say it is your turn."

(After a short time)

"Roy, one more minute, then it will be Pat's turn with the fire engine."

(Roy carries it to Pat.)

The feelings of each boy were expressed and understood. They were not told that they should not feel the way they did. I helped each of them hear the other's feeling in such a way that they could arrive at a dependable strategy of relationship. They both felt good about themselves after this experience. The boys started caring for each other. It was the beginning of being good friends.

There are definite steps in a child's processing of feelings.

Step 1: The feelings are verbalized by the child and by the significant adult so that the child understands his own feelings.

Step 2: In a social situation the child needs to hear the other child's feelings.

Step 3: The child works on a solution to the situation and brings it off, or the adult proposes a solution that the child can try.

The primary goal is not for the teacher to learn about the child. The important part is that the child comes to understand his own feelings, learns dependable ways of clarifying them, and solves the problem confronting him. A child needs to know that he is not alone with feelings that are overwhelming. He wants someone to hear him and enable him to come through even though it takes a struggle. He wants to come through as more of a person. The deep concern of the teacher is to enable a child to function with all that he has.

Being Understood by a Person Who Has Enabled the Child to Function

It has been our experience that the understanding has to come from a person who has previously enabled the child to function. The child then feels that person is on his side, and he will listen to the person's understanding, because it is valued.

On Friday of the first week of school, Mrs. Jones comes for her son Jack, and says that she is also to take Faye home. Faye becomes frightened and clings to me.

Mrs. S: "Faye, it bothers you to go home with someone else?"

Faye: "My mama."

Mrs. S: "You want your mother to come for you?"
(Faye nods yes.)
"Faye, your mother asked Jack's mother to bring you to your house. Your mother is waiting at your house. Jack's mother will take you to your house first."
(Faye goes willingly.)

From previous experiences of understanding, Faye was beginning to hear me. It was important that I verbalize her feelings. It helped her understand what was going on inside of her. Then she could listen to my interpretation of the situation. She could act. She was in charge of her behavior.

This handling of Faye's situation differs from methods suggested by some advocates of behavior modification. They recommend not paying attention to a child who cries and clings, erroneously reasoning that this "undesirable" behavior will be extinguished and that paying attention to it will encourage it. Ignoring would have neither stopped her crying nor helped her learn to take charge of her self. If Faye had not been helped to understand this situation that caused her intense anxiety, she would not have any increased ability to independently handle the next frightening situation. Not paying attention to her would only increase the stress she must cope with. Helping her understand her fears, and what the situation is really about, enabled her to trust and to take charge of herself.

The goal of the significant adult in this incident was to help Faye learn how to work her way through situations and become a self-propelling child rather than a teacher-directed or mother-directed child. Rather than treating Faye as a conglomerate of separate behavior patterns, I treated her as a person who can learn to integrate her feelings effectively.

We have confidence that there is a thrust toward growth in every child. And if he or she is treated as a person, each one will indeed grow.

UNDERSTANDING THE CHILD'S EXISTENCE SITUATION

The most productive level of understanding is catching the essence of a child's existence situation. This is more than just understanding feelings; it is understanding the child's total situation as a person as of that moment. It includes understanding the growing the child is working on and his or her struggle to build a desirable life world. It also includes what the child and the external world are doing to each other.

The Growing the Child is Working On

Some children are working on becoming able to initiate activity for themselves.

> Gerry is a very weak and helpless boy when he starts school. Most of his communication is crying. At first the cry seems to say, "I can't. Will someone please help me?" Then the cry changes to, "I want to play too, but I don't know how." One morning in December, Gerry is doing a great deal of whining. He stands in the middle of the room saying the same things over and over:
>
> > Gerry: "I want to paint. I want to paint."
> > Mrs. S: "You want to paint, Gerry, and you are having a hard time getting started?"

Understanding his desire and also what was blocking his action was enough to bring his confusion into focus. It made it possible for him to gain control of himself and take the initiative to walk to the easel and start to paint. It would not have helped to say, "You want to paint, Gerry," or "You are feeling weak, Gerry." He knew he wanted to paint but that wasn't all that he was feeling at that time. He had no experince in doing things for himself. His energies were not under his control. His way of meeting his needs in the past had been to cry, and this had brought immediate help. Previously he did not recognize the turmoil inside himself and failed to realize that he could take care of himself.

Some very disturbed children use their own private symbols when they are working at growing. Catching the essence of their existence situation helps the child think with socially understood symbols.

Four-year-old Zack is very weak and confused when he enters school. One day in February he is looking at a picture of a ship in the transportation book with a student teacher. A large seagull and two small ones are in the picture.

> Zack: "The little birds are the good birds."
> ST: "The little ones are good?"
> Zack: "Yes, but the big one is the bad bird."
> ST: "The big one is the bad one?"
> Zack: "Yes, but the little ones are going to get the best of the bad one."
> ST: "The little ones are going to get the best of the bad one?"
> Zack: "That's my mother."
> (Pointing to the big bird)
> ST: "The mean one is like your mother?"
> (The student's interpretation is too overwhelming.)
> Zack: "No."
> (He turns the page quickly.)

Up to the final reply the student teacher was helping Zack work on his problem, but then her conclusion was too startling. Suddenly he saw too clearly the Life World he had to deal with and it was too much. It would have been interesting if the student teacher had said, "Sometimes you feel that your mother is like that?" He probably would have been able to continue and then the student, knowing the mother, could have said, "You would like very much not to let it bother you when your mother gets so upset?" This is the existence situation that Zack was working on. The important part is not how he feels, but how he can handle his mother so that she does not overwhelm him.

One of the growings a child is working on is putting together a Life World.

On the first day of school we go outside to play. Most of the children want to ride the tricycles. Since we do not have as many tricycles as there are children, they have to take turns. When his turn is over and Robin has to give up the tricycle, he came to where I am sitting.

Robin: "You're a mean lady taking turns away from children."

Mrs. S: "You like the trike and didn't want to get off?"

Robin: "You shouldn't take it away from me. I'm going to kick you in the back."

Mrs. S: "It was hard for you to give up the trike? You wanted a longer turn?"

Robin: "Yes"

He stays around as if he wants to come back into relationship, so after a while:

Mrs. S: "How would you like to play ball?"

Robin: "Do you have a ball? I would like to play ball."

Robin was hot about having to give up his tricycle. At home, he had learned to express intense feelings. When he knew that I understood, he no longer needed to kick me. Expressing such anger to an adult could have left him anxious that he might have cut off relations with me. The fact that I received him and understood his anger rather than retaliating was very important, but in this case he needed another action. He needed some free invitation from me to restore our relationship. If I had said only, "You're mad at me for taking your trike away," it would not have been as helpful to him. My understanding of his intense desire to ride the tricycle longer made it possible for him to express his deeper desire for relationship.

The teacher needs to sense the situation of the child—the project he is trying to bring off—rather than simply respond to the outer manifestations of his feelings or of his words. Robin's feelings changed during the conversation. The teacher needs to be sensitive to the change and respond to it, or she may keep the child upset and make it harder for him to change.

Understanding the existence situation gets at the deep struggling self of a child. This is not easy and may take a long time. Continued trouble is a signal that there is a disturbance in the basic thrust of the child. Until this can be dealt with, the teacher will be working on surface manifestations.

> The children have stopped playing with Myra. She is an attractive girl who wants to play with other children, but the way she acts prevents relationships. She has developed very charming, sophisticated ways of controlling her younger sister and her mother. She always needs to establish herself in a domineering role; she has to control the world. Myra does not want to be treated like other children. She feels that if you really love her, you will give her special privileges.
>
> At toilet time one day, there is a line. Two children are waiting and one is on the toilet. Myra tries to get the corner spot where Matilda is waiting to be next. When Matilda protests, Myra tries to get in ahead of Rena, who also protests.

> | Mrs. S: | "Myra, Matilda and Rena have been waiting. You need to get in line." |
> |---|---|
> | Myra: | I'm going to tell my mother on you." |
> | | (My explanation had not helped, so I decide to show that I understand her and the others.) |
> | Mrs. S: | "Myra, you were in a hurry to get out to run. Rena and Matilda, you want to run too. You don't want Myra to get ahead of you when you have been waiting." |

> On another morning Jack wants to wash the doll with long hair. I explain to him that washing the doll's hair makes it get matted, and that it takes a long time to get it straightened out. He accepts another doll willingly. Myra hears this and wants to wash the one with the long hair.

> | Mrs. S: | "Myra, yesterday you did wash the dolly with the long hair. You tried hard not to get the hair wet, but even so it got wet and all matted up. I had a hard time trying to fix her hair this morning. Use this doll instead, please." |
> |---|---|
> | | (I hand her another, but she runs to her locker.) |

Myra: "I'm going to tell my mother you won't let me play with anything."

Mrs. S: "You liked washing her yesterday. But the water matted her hair, Myra."

Myra: "My mother lets me wash my dolls."

Mrs. S: "That is because they belong to you. This one belongs to the school and I can't let you do what I don't let others do."

(She seems to understand and no longer feels that she is being unfairly treated.)

Because of Myra's persistent attempts to dominate, the children do not enjoy playing with her. We verbalized their feelings, hoping that Myra will become sensitive to them, but her despair prevents her from allowing herself to feel for them. They are only things to her. One day Myra is absent. At toilet time this conversation takes place.

Mrs. S: "Myra isn't here today. I hope she isn't sick."

Matilda: "I don't like Myra."

Rena: "We don't like her."

Mrs. S: "Myra did something you don't like?"

Matilda: "When I went to her house, she wouldn't let me play with her things. She hit me."

Mrs. S: "It isn't very much fun to go to someone's house and she doesn't let you play with her toys?"

Rena: "She did it to me, too."

Mrs. S: "I am trying to help Myra learn to play so it will be fun."

Matilda: "Then we made cookies at her house."

Mrs. S: "Then that was fun."

Matilda: "Yes, and we brought some to school."

Mrs. S: "They were good cookies."

They seem to feel good about this conversation. I am trying to help them separate what they do not like from not liking in general. I want them to be able to tell her when she offends them.

When the other children begin to hold their own at play, Myra feels she is losing out. She can no longer control or dominate the play, she becomes fragile. When things do not work out, she runs to her locker where she feels sorry for herself and waits for someone to come and love her back into being. But it is a being who cannot accept the others as selves with feelings.

Myra is at the point where her behavior does not help her play with other children. A child like Myra needs to work through her anxieties about being abandoned. She is afraid that she will lose out unless she controls the world, because, as she sees it, that is her only way to get what she needs. She is demanding that we let her do as she pleases.

With Myra we feel it is important not to confirm and intensify the feeling that she is about to be abandoned or to give her the feeling that she is undesirable. The inappropriate behavior should not pay off. We need to be careful not to turn Myra back on herself but toward relationship.

We try to reinforce her desire to play and build up her ego strength with successful experiences. Gradually she wants to stay in relationship. Then starts the long process of helping her stay in relationship. One morning I am with some children who are washing the wall in the bathroom. Myra comes running to me crying.

Mrs. S: "Myra, something is wrong?"

Myra: "Matilda hit me. She won't let me in the house."

Mrs. S: "You were playing with her and then she hit you?"

Myra: "I helped build the house and she won't let me in."

Mrs. S: "Well, we better go talk to Matilda."
(We go to her.)

Mrs. S: "Matilda, Myra says you hit her."

Matilda: "She knocked down my baby and she can't do that."

Mrs. S: "Oh, she knocked down your baby, and you were telling her hard not to knock down your baby."
(This makes Myra retreat to the window ledge. I go to her.)

Mrs. S: "Myra, Matilda didn't want you to hurt her baby."
(She puts her hands over her ears.)
"You don't want to talk about it anymore?"
(I turn to leave, thinking that she wants to think it over, but when she starts to cry loudly I go back to her.)

	"You wanted me to help you but I haven't helped you?"
Myra:	"I didn't knock down Matilda's baby. I bumped Matilda and she did."
Mrs. S:	"You didn't mean to bump Matilda. If you had told her, Matilda would understand that you did not mean to do it. Maybe if we tell her now she will understand."
	(She does not seem able to do this.)
Mrs. S:	"If you want me to go with you, I will help you."
	(We go to Matilda.)
Mrs. S:	"Matilda, Myra said that she bumped you but didn't mean to."
Matilda:	"I'm fixing the steps and she can come in the steps."
	(Myra is happy to get in again. Unfortunately, she accidentally knocks down the wall
Mrs. S:	"Oh, oh, those steps are difficult to get up. We need to fix the wall again."
	(I helped Matilda rebuild the wall. It does not bother her when she knows it was an accident.)

This had been a dark moment for Myra. She had been hit and put out of the house that she had helped build, by the girl she valued most. But she could not connect this rejection with the cause. Matilda could only strike out when her baby was violated. I enabled them to talk together until they understood each other and could come back into relationship. In the process, the two girls became integrities dealing with each other.

Nursery school is a place where both teacher and the child work on understanding the growing the child is trying to bring off and the kind of Life World she is struggling for. Always a child has a project going—a livable world which she is building with the world around her. Often it is a partially muddled or mistaken goal; both her intentions and her methods of working have to be refelt and a better way found. By the process of mutual understanding with those involved, the child becomes able to affirm a possible world, learns how to bring it off, and understands what defeats it. Also, the child can celebrate when she succeeds.

RECONSTRUCTING THE EPISODE WITH FEELINGS AND INTENTIONS

A teacher reconstructs the episode when she enters a conflict situation and goes over with the children the chain of events, including the feelings and intentions of those involved. Helping the group relive the situation has to be done by the adult in such a way that it is an "offering" and not an attempt to force one particular interpretation upon the children. Otherwise, the children will not feel free to correct the teacher's understanding if she is wrong. This is why replies of understanding are often given with a questioning inflection in the voice and questions marks are used in some of the book's dialogues. You are not sure that you really captured the child's feeling. You are offering a way of seeing what happened, not telling a child how it happened or probing. You are open to either confirmation or correction.

Reconstructing an episode with the feelings and intentions combines all three of the other forms of understanding, in addition to a retracing of the events in the present conflict.

Early in the school year, Trudy is fragile. Her family has been living in a motel for four months, waiting for their new house to be finished. All of her familiar things are in storage. At nursery school, she keeps trying to put her world back together.

One morning she discovers the small outdoor cupboard in which the tricycles are kept. She gets the big broom and starts sweeping and cleaning the cupboard. This looks like fun to Ted, who is used to taking what he wants and building up a head of steam quickly if his intentions are blocked. Ted tries to take her broom, but Trudy fights hard to hold onto it.

Mrs. S:	"Trudy, you were cleaning your house. It's such a nice house."
Trudy:	(Crying) "He can't have it. He can't come in."
Mrs. S:	"Ted, it looks like fun to be in Trudy's house and to sweep the dirt out of here, so that it can be your house too."
Ted:	(Puffing hard) "I want it."

Mrs. S: "Ted, you would like to sweep the house too, and you don't know how you can get the broom except to take it away from Trudy?"

Ted: "Yes."

Mrs. S: "Ted, if Trudy says 'no,' you can tell me that you want a turn with the broom and I would see that you get it as soon as Trudy's turn is over."

Trudy: "He can have it, but I want it back."

Mrs. S: "All right, Ted, Trudy says that you may use it now. Trudy, I will tell Ted when his turn is over."

Both of these children had intense feelings that were beyond their own control. Hearing me voice Trudy's intentions and feelings helped her know what was happening to her; she also knew it was all right to feel upset, and Ted was helped to see how much the broom meant to Trudy. My voicing his desire let Ted know that it was all right to want the broom, so he was free to listen to how to get it. Trudy also could feel Ted's desire for the broom and she could part with it, at least temporarily, if she knew she could get it back. When I entered the situation I had intended only to help Ted wait for his turn by helping him understand how much the broom meant to Trudy. In the process, more was made possible. Reconstructing an episode with the feelings and intentions included helps children learn to care for each other.

Understanding a child is not just for the purpose of handling a particular episode. It is a long-term strategy of helping a child to accurately perceive the situations he is in and acquire a style of feeling his world. It also makes available words and action models with which to organize a meaningful world, and to present it to himself and others in such a way that all involved can live understandingly.

Furthermore, repeated experiences with an understanding adult and peers help the child develop an inner poise so that he no longer panics or turns to irrational behavior when he faces trouble and conflicts. He has learned another mode of dealing with the world and himself.

With experience, a teacher can tell which level of understanding to use. Often, verbal content alone is enough. When a child is fearful or withdrawn, the feeling level is needed, and sometimes the existence situation. When two or more children are having trouble, reliving the situation with stress on the feelings of each is the most helpful.

Not even an experienced teacher can understand all of the time. One learns from mistakes, then tries harder the next time.

Understanding is important. It is one of a cluster of essential methods we use with children.

Chapter 7

THE ART OF UNDERSTANDING

Power to understand is crucial professional equipment for the nursery school teacher—and for parents. This chapter is written for those who want to improve their skill in understanding. Practice and discipline are necessary, especially to reach the most productive levels. Anyone can learn, but understanding is very complex; one must grasp not only the child's words and feelings, but also the levels of existence and sometimes total episodes.

Understanding as possessed by a professional has a precise meaning. It is a particular skill that is more than what most people would call understanding. It should not be confused with listening passively or with being merely agreeable or forgiving.

NOT UNDERSTANDING

There are many kinds of replies that prevent understanding and stop the child's own problem-solving process.

Some replies that prevent understanding are probing, instructing, evaluating, and supporting. Three others—changing the topic, not responding at all, and arguing—will not be described since they are obvious.

Probing

Probing is an attempt to get someone to reveal the past or the reasons for her behavior. It is based on the assumption that once answers are known, the problem will be solved. When questions take the form "why did you do it," they are often intended to make a child feel or admit guilt. Attempts to get information often defeat the process of understanding.

Children close up fast when asked direct questions. Probing is apt to cause children to force feelings down inside, where they become very difficult to deal with. Children rightly feel that the adult is trying to control or blame them, rather than helping them function, so they conclude that it is dangerous to disclose feelings and let other people hear their thoughts. Probing disturbs inner speech.

Probing is a poor technique because it may change a child's line of thought or cause a child to become evasive or defensive. We never know which way a child will go. It is important to follow her lead rather than force her in the wrong direction by questions that make it more difficult for her to stay on the track. The teacher who starts asking questions has given up understanding.

Instructing

Instructing tells a person what to do or unnecessarily explains something. Instructing a child insinuates that she is not capable of thinking for herself and that she needs an adult to take over. Hence the child becomes weaker, and she may learn to depend on someone else's thinking.

Children stop listening when someone is always telling them what to do or is giving them unnecessary facts. Instructing makes the adult feel important, but it robs the child of her independence. It is completely different from explaining something that the child wants to understand.

Evaluating

Evaluating puts a value judgment on an act or places an interpretation on it. It attempts to coerce behavior by saying "this is good" or "this is bad." Such remarks prevent the child from arriving at the truth. She is apt instead to try to please adults. Interpreting an act according to the teacher's values may exclude other possible courses of the child's behavior and shut off the expression of feeling. Negative critical evaluations destroy self-esteem and cause defensiveness. Truth will be a more potent force in the child's life if she has had a chance to arrive at her own judgments through her own experience and thinking.

Supporting

Supporting tries to make a person feel good and encourages evasion of the real issue. It tries to substitute "good" feelings for unacceptable ones, to deny the reality of them, or to distract the child. The message the child receives is, "You really shouldn't feel the way you do." When a person is in trouble, comments such as, "You're all right," "Everyone goes through this," and "You are such a good boy," offer a false kind of support.

Supportive replies prevent a child from working through the problem, and cause a great deal of inner confusion. Telling a child that what he is feeling is not so, or that he should not feel that way, confuses the child and leaves him unable to help himself. How can a child know reality if he is not allowed to feel it? Here is an illustration of this false support, the kind that hurts rather than helps a child.

> One morning during singing the children begin to criticize Frank for not singing right. He is shouting the words but not singing the tune.

> Mrs. S: "Frank, it would sound prettier if you would sing the tune with the rest of us."
> Frank: "But I am singing."
> Mrs. S: "You're saying the words, Frank, but try to sing the tune along with us."
> Frank: "That's not the way you sing. My mother says I'm a very good singer."

> Later, when I had a chance to talk to his mother alone, I asked what she had told Frank about his singing. She commented, "Oh yes, we tell him he's a good singer so that we don't hurt his feelings. He's cute, but he really can't sing."

Frank's mother thought she was being kind and supportive by telling Frank he was a good singer, but her compliments built up a false sense of competence and put him in a very embarrassing situation. His mother was only adding to Frank's confusion. Frank needed to have an honest report from his mother. It would also have helped if his mother had tried to teach him to sing properly instead of encouraging "cute" incompetence.

There may not be anything wrong with these four kinds of replies when you are not trying to understand. But if you use them, you need to know that you are not understanding, even at a superficial level.

PRACTICE IN UNDERSTANDING

When illustrations of understanding are read, they seem obvious and easy to do. But when one has to figure out what to say in a live situation or when the answer is not given, one realizes that this is a skill requiring work and practice. We have found the following exercise of writing out replies very helpful. When you come to the line marked xxxxx, first write replies that are probing, instructing, evaluating, and supporting. Then write the understanding reply. This will help distinguish real understanding from its inauthentic forms. Then examine the answers that are given.

While playing in the sand box, Rick tries to reach deep into the hole he has dug and kicks Sarah in the mouth, making it bleed. She is crying hard.

Mrs. S:	"It hurts a lot, Sarah?"
Sarah:	"Yes."
Mrs. S:	"It is bleeding some."
Sarah:	"I want my mother."
Your reply:	xxxxx

Probing replies: "Did you do something to Rick's hole?" "Why do you want your mother, Sarah?"

Instructing replies: "Go in and wash your face." "Rick, tell Sarah you're sorry for making her nose bleed."

Evaluating replies: "That was a mean thing that Rick did to you, kicking you in the mouth." "Stop crying. It didn't hurt you that much." "Rick, why did you hurt Sarah?"

Supporting replies: "You're a big girl now. The bleeding will stop in a little bit." "I'm sure it was an accident, Sarah."

Understanding: Reply: "When you get hurt, it helps to be with your mother?"

This last reply was the one that was used. Sarah recovered from her fear. In the rest of the episode, I was giving her information to help her understand the experience.

Sarah: "Yes."

Mrs. S: "It is beginning to stop bleeding, Sarah. It may hurt a little longer, but it will be all right."

This experience involves a three-year-old girl learning to adjust to the world away from home. Sometimes the understanding method is slower than getting the episode over as fast as possible. But it gives the child a chance to work through her feelings. And she knows the teacher is for her-understandingly.

Robin is a bright four-year-old with a great deal of ability. Lately he has been displaying the interests of an engineer. His paintings depict the insides of factories, boats, and airplanes.

One morning he is building a big ship, combining our big green box, a long plank, and the top of our block cupboard. He wants the plank fastened onto the box in a special way, but it will not hold. Nothing is working right. I am trying my best to put the big plank where he wants it, but he starts to cry.

Robin: "Mrs. Snyder, you go away. I don't want you here."

Your
response: xxxxx

Probing: "What's the matter, Robin?" "Why do you get so upset when things don't work out right?"

Instructing: "Robin, some things just won't work."

Supporting: "You are a bright boy, Robin. You can do it."

Evaluating: "Robin, if you quit whining we could get it done."

Understanding: "The boat just isn't the way you want it to be and you want me to let you work on it yourself."

Robin's reaction to my response was interesting. I left, but he followed me into the other room and kept talking to me about boats. Understanding helped him handle his frustrations. It also helped to build a trusting relationship between us.

As student teachers are learning to make understanding replies to children's statements, they make some common mistakes. The next episode demonstrates some of these mistakes, and shows why these replies are not understanding.

One night it rained hard. There was loud thunder and lightning. The next day Cliff's mother says he was afraid. At juice time I start to talk about the storm.

Mrs. S:	"That was a noisy old storm last night."
Malcolm:	"It kept me awake. The lightning made a loud noise and I was afraid."
Sally:	"I was scared too, when the big noise came."
Dean:	"It was like a big gun and I didn't like it."
Cliff:	"When the loud noise came, it could knock down the houses."
Your response:	xxxxx

Here are some replies that students have made when learning to respond with understanding.

1. "Cliff, it was so loud you thought it might knock down your house?" This reply is close to a correct interpretation, but it jumps to a conclusion and prevents Cliff from working it through himself. And, it may be partially incorrect, since he did not say it might destroy his house.
2. "Lightning is very powerful." This is a factual statement about lightning that does not come to terms with Cliff's feelings or fears. In fact, it may confirm his fear. This response does not capture the fact that Cliff was responding to the force of the noise.
3. "Lightning doesn't usually strike houses." This is an instructing and supportive response that tries to make Cliff believe what is said and not be scared. It is better to understand his feelings so that he can continue to

work on his fears and so that he will be more open to an explanation later.

4. "The storm got over and your house wasn't struck." This is the student's conclusion, stated in a supportive manner. Fears are overcome faster if the child can work with his feelings in the presence of an adult who can help him face these feelings.

5. "I know how you feel. It was scary enough to knock down houses." Telling a child you know how he feels is not the same as being able to put his feelings into words in such a way that he experiences your understanding. The first sentence is therefore unnecessary. The second sentence is one possible interpretation. Another would be that Cliff was awe-struck with the power of the sound, and was not primarily responding with fear. Again, the student's interpretation stops the child's internal processing.

6. "It was so loud, you thought it might knock down houses?" This is a good, understanding reply, especially when conveyed in a manner that responds to the child's intensity of feeling. I responded, "The lightning was very bright and the thunder very loud."

This started them all talking again. Then later, I began to provide information that they needed to understand the realities of lightning and thunder.

Sally:	"It burns up houses."
Mrs. S:	"Not very often, Sally."
Bob:	"Sometimes the lightning strikes trees and that's why you don't stay under them."
Cliff:	"Will it strike our tree?"
Mrs. S:	"Our tree has been here a long, long time and it hasn't been struck. But we would come inside if it started to lightning and thunder, because sometimes lightning does strike tall trees."

Here are some more episodes. When you come to xxxxx, cover up my replies before reading on and write down your understanding reply. There is no need to practice the other types of replies.

> One morning I am sitting on the floor next to Sam building with blocks. He speaks to me in a matter of fact way:

Sam:	"Mrs. Snyder, I go to bed with a bottle at night."
Your reply:	xxxxx
Mrs. S:	"Sam, you want me to know you go to bed with a bottle?"
Sam:	"Yes, but when I get to be four, I'm not going to anymore."
Mrs. S:	"When you get to be four, you are going to stop."
Sam:	"Yes."

Here is a bright boy working out his future. I could have muddled his thinking by making him feel guilty. Giving him advice would also have complicated the situation.

> One morning Carol is playing in the sandbox and Dennis hits her with a plastic shovel. Carol comes to me crying. She is emotionally broken up.

Carol:	"Dennis hit me with a spoon, Mrs. Snyder."
Your reply:	xxxxx
Mrs. S:	"Dennis hurt you and you don't know why?" She turns and immediately goes back to play.

Carol was confused about something that had happened to her that did not make sense. She could not understand the situation she was in. Why would Dennis hit her? Often a child's feelings are complex. Voicing the two strands of Carol's feelings helped her so that she could take over again. It gave her courage to continue.

On another occasion I am reading and Carol comes up to me.

Carol:	"I want that fire engine that Abe is playing with."
Mrs. S:	"You know, Carol, when you want something, you ask the person if you may have it. You say that you would like to have a turn with it."
Carol:	"But he may say 'no.'"
Your reply:	xxxxx

Mrs. S:	"It would be hard to know what to do if he said 'no.'"
Carol:	(Meaning she would not know) "No."
Mrs. S:	"Sometimes when you ask people, they do say 'no,' and then you just wait until they are finished."
Carol:	"But Abe won't finish. He will want it a long time."
Mrs. S:	"If Abe says 'no,' then you can tell me and I will tell Abe he may have three minutes more and then it will be your turn." (My saying three minutes is an objective way of saying a short time. It then becomes a matter of the watch saying so, and Carol won't feel that begging me will help her get the fire engine sooner.)

You notice that in my first reply I thought that just explaining was enough. But when Carolyn said "He may say 'no,'" understanding was needed. There seemed to be something keeping her from accepting the explanation. It turned out that she would not know what to do if the person said "no."

Now try using the four levels of understanding that we use in our nursery school.

Understanding Verbal Content

Ann is playing that she is going on a picnic with some children. She comes to me.

Ann:	"We just can't find the hot dogs anywhere!"
Your reply:	xxxxx

Mrs. S:	"A picnic and no hot dogs?" (She goes off in a dither and then comes back.)
Ann:	"We even called the chef and he doesn't know."
Your reply:	xxxxx

Mrs. S:	"Not even the chef knows?" (She leaves again and returns once more.)
Ann:	"We found the hot dogs."
Mrs. S:	"Good, I'm glad of that."
Ann:	"You know where we found the hot dogs?"
Mrs. S:	"No. Where?"
Ann:	"In the car. They were on the seat all the time."
Mrs. S:	"That was a good joke on you, wasn't it?" (We both laugh.)

In this episode I started by understanding, but as I began to sense the fun she was having I contributed to it. Relationships are more than just understanding. A nursery school teacher should not become fixed on one mode of relationship.

Hearing and Processing Feelings

In the following episode, concentrate on the feelings as well as the words.

Anita is still wearing her corrective shoes, but outside in the playground she is quite free. She climbs up the new ladders on our trailer, but coming down she slips on the last two steps. I did not think that she had hurt herself so I exclaimed, "Oh-o," to see if I could help her take her bumps.

Anita:	"I almost broke my leg."
Your reply:	xxxxx

Mrs. S:	"It seemed hard enough to break your leg?"
Anita:	"Yes, I almost broke my leg."

She starts to laugh and we laugh together. Then she returns to climbing the steps but she jumps off the last two steps on the way down.

Understanding the Existence Situation

In these examples listen to the words, get the feelings, and try to understand what the child is working on. (You are trying to understand all three of these at once.)

Trudy has one younger brother named David, and she has been bringing some of her toys to school and keeping them in her locker so that her brother cannot get at them. One morning in the coat room when the children are getting ready to go home, Trudy is putting on her coat. She seems happy.

Trudy: "I have four brothers. David, David, and David. David are both older and David are younger."
Your reply: xxxxx

ST: "You have four brothers, Trudy, and they are all named David?"
Trudy: "Yes, all named David. Two are older and two are younger."
Your reply: xxxxx

The student teacher stopped because she could not figure out where to go. She had been responding to Trudy's words. If she had grasped the dilemma of Trudy's existence, she might have said, "Sometimes living with David is like having four brothers." Then Trudy could have taken it from there. It had been a good morning at school. A morning when she was feeling good might have been the best time for her to work out her relationship with a strong and energetic brother.

This is another episode in which the existence situation needs to be understood.

Cliff is playing alone with an airplane and has made an airport for it out of blocks on the floor. I am sitting close by.

| Cliff: | "I don't want to ride in an airplane again." |
| Your reply: | xxxxx |

Mrs. S:	"It was scary, Cliff?"
Cliff:	"No, it was noisy. I don't like airplanes."
Your reply:	xxxxx

Mrs. S:	"The one you were in made lots of noise?" (Pause) "Sometimes airplanes make a lot of noise just before they go up. They want to be sure the motors are working."
Cliff:	"It went up high, above the clouds and above the trees, and above the houses."
Your reply:	xxxxx

Mrs. S:	"It seemed very high to you?"
Cliff:	"That was when my grandmother died." (Here I remembered that his grandmother, whom he loved very much, had died a month ago and his family had gone east to bury her.)
Your reply:	xxxxx

Mrs. S:	"Your grandmother was very kind, wasn't she? She is dead now."
Cliff:	"I won't see her anymore."
Your reply:	xxxxx

| Mrs. S: | "It is hard not to see your grandmother any-more?" |

Cliff had associated the noise of the airplane with the unsettling death of his grandmother. He was having a difficult time accepting her death. By understanding his existence situation at this time, I was trying to help him accept his grandmother's death. In my first response, I mistakenly made an interpretation in trying to understand him. He was fast to correct me. A better reply would have been, "There is something you don't like about airplanes?" In a good relationship, the child will feel free to correct you when you are wrong.

Reconstructing the Episode With Feelings and Intentions

In these examples use all three of the previous levels of understanding, but also try to relive the developing situation with the children. Try to make your response in the feeling tones of an offering rather than in a tone which suggests that you are offering the only interpretation.

> During the second week of school, Tom, who had been very rough, is beginning to learn how to play with other children. Clarice is a four-year-old girl who had not played with boys before coming to school. She pulls her wagon next to the jungle gym where the boys are playing, and in a timid voice, calls out to get one of them to pull her.

> | Clarice: | "Who will pull me?" |
> |---|---|
> | | (They do not pay any attention to her.) |
> | Mrs. S: | "Clarice is asking if someone will pull her in the wagon." |
> | Tom: | "I will, I will." |

Clarice gets into the wagon and Tom pulls. They start off around the sidewalk, circling the tree. Tom picks up speed. Clarice enjoys it at first, but when he starts going too fast around the curves, she becomes frightened. She tries to get out. Tom is disappointed because he thought they were having fun, so he tries to keep her in the wagon by going faster.

> Your reply: xxxxx

> | Mrs. S: | "Tom, it is fun pulling Clarice. Clarice, you liked having Tom pull you until he got going too fast. Then you thought the wagon might tip going so fast?" |
> |---|---|

Clarice climbs out of the wagon. Tom seems disappointed. Then his face brightens and he looks at Clarice.

Tom: "Will someone pull me?"
Clarice: "I will."

They pull each other for the rest of the period.

By reliving the situation the children could recapture the fun of what they were doing. When I put into words what caused the change in Clarice's feelings, she was able to overcome her fear. When she knew that Tom understood her concern, she did not have to stop playing with him. Tom had enjoyed playing with Clarice, so now he invited her to continue by saying to her, "Will someone pull me?" He did not need to say he was sorry. She understood and responded with, "I will." After pulling him for a while they traded and he pulled her again. This time Tom was more careful about the turns.

Chapter 8

HOW UNDERSTANDING HELPS THE CHILD

Having looked at the different forms of understanding, we can now pull together the growing made possible by a teacher who is skilled in understanding. Most importantly, conversation that leads to understanding another person is a major way in which we become a person and create a society that can live together, by which values can be shared and created across generations.

We have found that understanding helps the child in many specific ways.

GIVES THE CHILD RELATIONSHIP AND WORDS WITH WHICH TO IDENTIFY FEELINGS AND CONTROL ACTIONS

Sometimes children are overwhelmed by a lot of confused feelings. A child needs help in learning accurate words for her feelings and for the confusion around her. She then can make choices and discover what relationships she really wants.

Dee is an active four-year-old girl who in the midst of play will say, "I'm mad," putting one hand on her hip and stamping her foot. Often the children would give way and let her have her way. One day, while playing in the housekeeping corner, she throws her doll on the floor.

Dee:	(Hand on hip and stamping her foot) "I'm mad." (She kicks the doll across the room.)
Mrs. S:	(Picking up the doll and talking to it) "Sally, you must feel bad having a mother be so mean to you just because she is mad. Maybe you would like some dinner?"
	(I take the doll to the table where others are playing. They start to share their pretend food with me and the doll.)
Dee:	"I will feed her, Mrs. Snyder."
Mrs. S:	"All right,
	(I hand her the doll and she takes it with tenderness.)

In the next week Dee is drawing a picture at the table with magic markers.

Mrs. S:	"That's an interesting picture, Dee."
Dee:	"This is my house. This is the door where you come in. That's the living room. But this is the hall. You go this way. This is the room where I sleep and my sister sleeps. That is my mother and dad's room. They have the door closed so the children won't hear them fighting."
Mrs. S:	"You don't like to hear your mother and father fighting?"
Dee:	"No."
Mrs. S:	"It is hard to live with people who fight when they feel mean?"
Dee:	"Yes."

Hearing parents trying to destroy each other is a terrible experience for a four-year-old. Dee was trying to play out the experience by putting some of the feelings onto the doll so that the pressure would not be just on her. When I voiced the feelings of the doll, she recognized that this treatment was not right. By sharing in a conversation with a person who understood, she had entered into another relationship. She was taken into society, rather than being trapped with a horrible memory. This helped her face how it upset her, and how people feel when treated the way her parents were treating each other. She could say to herself, "I don't like that. I don't have to be that." She was becoming able to make feeling judgments.

Something is hidden in most unpleasant experiences that the person involved does not recognize. It drives the person, rather than allowing growth. The significant adult hears and knows what has happened, and the child now knows that she does. But the adult is not devastated by the situation. The child now has a new hold on the experience.

These two experiences with Sue are illustrations of how terribly important understanding is in the life of a child. It helps her shape up a method and a vocabulary with which to feelingly think, make value judgments, and to govern her behavior.

STRENGTHENS THE CHILD'S POWER TO ACT

Ivan is a four-year-old boy who is very withdrawn when he starts school. His eyes have a glassy look and he drools profusely. He is silent most of the time, and when he does talk, he speaks in a whisper.

In January I put out a new set of miniature cars. The other children play with them with real excitement. Ivan watched closely. After a while he comes to where I am sitting on the window seat. One of the new yellow road builders is next to me.

Ivan: (Softly, looking longingly at it) "That's a road
         builder."
         (I picked it up and put it in the palm of my
         hand.)

Mrs. S: "I believe that it would smooth out the dirt and make a good road."

I hope that he will take it. Ivan looks, but cannot reach out to get it. I put it down on the window seat close to him. Just then another boy comes by and takes it. Ivan looks longingly at it as it disappears.

Mrs. S: "You wanted to play with it, Ivan? You didn't want Leo to take it?"

Ivan: "Yes."

Mrs. S: "You wanted it, but it was hard to reach out and get it?"

Ivan: "Yes."

Later that morning he comes up and speaks to me in a soft voice.

Ivan: "The red truck, Mrs. Snyder."

Mrs. S: "You want the little red truck, Ivan? I don't know where it is. We will have to find it."

He takes me to the housekeeping corner and points to the red truck on the play cabinet.

Ivan: "Here."

Mrs. S: "That's it, Ivan, and no one is playing with it."

Ivan takes it and goes off to play with it.

It took five months of experiences like this to help Ivan become free enough to take the playthings he wanted. It was interesting that the drooling disappeared at about the same time that he became able to do this.

Ivan had been very fearful of extending himself into the world. He had a need to ask permission and a custom of getting other people to do things for him. The function of the nursery school teacher was not to do things for him, or to urge him "to do" things, but to engage him in understanding coversations that made clearer and more intense what he wanted to do and at the same time affirm him. Finally the desire to play won out over his fears.

HELPS THE CHILD RECOVER FROM SETBACKS

If a child is understood by just one person, he can take a lot. He does not need to feel that he is disintegrating or that he must become destructive to survive. He can take some irritations in stride.

One morning as the children are arriving in the coat room, they start to make up songs.

Sam: "I have a new pillow.
My mother bought it from the store.
It is a nice new pillow.
Tra la, la, la, la."
Mrs. S: "That is such a nice song you are singing, Sam."
Sam: "You are interrupting me, Mrs. Synder."
Mrs. S: "I'm sorry, Sam. Your song was so pretty that I wanted to say so."
Sam: "Does Carol like it?"
Mrs. S: "You will have to ask her to find out."
Sam: "Do you like my song, Carol?"
Carol: "No, I don't like it."

With this, I go into the nursery school. When Sam comes in, he goes to Mrs. Martin, the other teacher, and says something. Then he picks up the paper towels and strews them over the floor.

Mrs. M: "Sam, you are angry about something?"
Sam: "Yes, I'm angry."
Mrs. M: "Sam, it doesn't help to throw things on the floor. Will you help me pick them up?"
Sam: "No, I'm angry."

Sam comes over to the books and is going to throw them down.

> Mrs. S: "Sam, you are angry on the inside and you want to do things you shouldn't do?"
>
> Sam: "Yes."
>
> Mrs. S: "You didn't like hearing Carol say that she did not like your song?"
>
> Sam: "No."
>
> Mrs. S: "You would have liked for her to like your song?"
>
> Sam: "Yes."

Here is a boy with a lot of explosive feelings; he could become destructive very easily. But because he has such a lively mind, his future is bright if we can help him learn to handle such feelings.

Even though he was angry, he knew that I was with him. Having someone hear and verbalize his feelings and yet accept him enabled him to recognize these feelings and not to be so upset by them. Mrs. Martin had not seen the episode in the coat room. She could only respond to Sam's throwing the towels. Her reply was too general to give him the precise help he needed, but it started the process. A child needs to know what produced his anger.

Sam also needs help in establishing relationships, not only with me, but also with Carol, who must be a significant person in his world. Here is another episode that happened after the first one.

Sam comes in singing.

> Sam: "Mrs. Snyder, do you like my singing?"
>
> Mrs. S: "Yes, Sam, that is a pretty song."
>
> Sam: "Where is Carol? Carol, do you like my song?"
>
> Carol: "No."

This time he walks away, evidently undisturbed.

Because he had a relationship with me, he was able to hold onto the relationship with himself, and then he was able to handle a relationship with another child.

GIVES THE CHILD'S HOPES AND PLANS A CHANCE

When a child is living in an over-controlled (or a too chaotic) world, a door opens to freedom and health when he is understood by someone who cares. He begins to trust that another kind of world is possible.

> Bob is a four-year-old who carries a heavy load of hostility. His mother is sick so he is living with his grandparents, who love him very much but are overprotective.
> One morning in the yard of the nursery school, Bob is throwing stones that are lying near a big tree.
>
> Mrs. S: "Bob, you might hurt someone, throwing those stones."
> Bob: "But I want to hurt people."
> Mrs. S: "When you feel mean on the inside, you want to hurt people?"
> Bob: "Yes."
>
> The tension seems to go out of him. His hands relax and the stones drop to the ground.

One episode like this is not enough to make a difference, but a series of them over the year is helpful. Here is another episode.

> Bob's grandmother stops at the door of the nursery school to tell me that it is Bob's birthday. She says that she will bring some cookies for juice time. Bob starts to play.
>
> (To me alone) "Bob is very negative about his birthday. He doesn't want anybody to know. He justs wants to keep it inside him."

The other children have not arrived, so I go to Bob.

Mrs. S:	"Bob, I will whisper a secret to you."
Bob:	"What?"
Mrs. S:	"Happy Birthday."
	(He smiles, then catches himself.)
Bob:	"No, don't tell anyone."
Mrs. S:	"All right."

When getting ready for juice time, I take Bob aside and ask him if he wants to put the candles in the animal holders. Bob gets a queer look on his face.

Bob:	"I don't want any singing or any candles."
Mrs. S:	"All right, you don't want us to sing 'Happy Birthday.' "
Bob:	"No."
Mrs. S:	"And you don't want us to light candles?"
Bob:	"No."
Mrs. S:	"All right. Do you want to pass the cookies?"
Bob:	"Yes."

So he passes the cookies and no one asks any questions. The next morning his grandmother thanks me for Bob's happy birthday. He told them at home that he didn't need any more birthday, that he had his happy birthday at school.

This episode also illustrates that understanding involves granting a child's request when it is appropriate, rather than just letting him voice his opposition and then igoring it.

DEVELOPS HONEST INNER SPEECH

Understanding may be used by the teacher to voice what the teacher senses the child is saying in his inner speech. This enables the child to review what he is saying to himself. The teacher is also offering the child possible words that may become part of his inner speech. She may be offering or sharing an insight into the nature of things that he is himself experiencing. By offering such insights, the teacher must not try to manipulate the child to do what she wants; she has to try to enter the child's thinking process in such a way that it allows the child to stay in charge.

BUILDS CONSCIENCE

Being understood and dialogued with is the basic tool in awakening a child's conscience and helping it function in a person-producing way. "Understanding conversation" helps the child to take account of his world and symbolize it with some fullness. It sometimes gives the child the necessary feedback that enables him to break through the fog or turmoil that has kept him on dead center. He comes to know what is going on inside himself. He can see his world. His perceptions and feelings get a new clarity. He is able to function at top performance. He is more alive.

This is a good feeling. He begins to care for the person who makes him feel this way. When he hears the teacher verbalize other children's feelings, he starts caring for them, because each one is another self with feelings.

SUMMARY

Being understood is very important to a child. Gradually the child begins to understand himself. When his feelings are expressed in symbols, he is able to stand above them, reorder, and organize them. He can work as an organizer of himself and is not taken over by his flood of emotions.

When his inner world is understood by a significant adult, he feels that he is accepted by society. He is kept from being estranged or shut up.

The public understanding of how it is with him is heard by the other children. They know better what is happening and what they can do to help. We are always amazed at how three- and four-year-olds can help each other when they understand what is happening.

Understanding is trusting the nature of creation, believing that a child will eventually choose the good, if he is given the chance to work it through.

Understanding is a basic tool for helping the growth and functioning of conscience.

In our understanding of a child, we are shaping a model of how people relate to each other. In the process of being understood, the child learns to go about understanding the people he must deal with. He acquires a method of growing intellectually and emotionally.

Chapter 9

AN INTEGRITY THAT CAN BE ENCOUNTERED

A major function of a teacher in the nursery school is to be an integrity that can be encountered.

By the age of three, some children already carry a heavy load of hostility. On some mornings such a child gets caught in a chain of events that makes him bitter and resentful. He does something to another child and gets rejected, and this rejection piles up with additional events until he wants to hurt and destroy everybody.

There is a right time to bring conflict out into the open and face it. A child needs to face his destructive actions. He needs to know that he cannot hurt someone else, or break up their play, even if he is feeling mean himself.

One morning Hubert picks another child off a tricycle and rides away with it. This happens so fast that the eye could hardly record it. Suddenly Hubert has the tricycle and Ted is on the ground crying. Mrs. Martin, the other teacher, goes to Hubert.

Mrs. M: "Hubert, you made Ted very unhappy by taking his trike. You will have to give it back to him."
(No response.)

Mrs. M: "Hubert, it was Ted's turn and you will have to give it back to him."
(No response.)

Mrs. M: "Hubert, if you don't get off I will have to take you off."

She tries to take him off the trike, but he clings tight. I go to help her. As soon as I do, Hubert jumps off and starts kicking me.

Mrs. S: "Hubert, that hurts, stop kicking me."

He backs up to get a running start and runs and kicks me again. This time I catch his foot and spill him.

Mrs. S: "That hurts, Hubert. Stop it."

He tries to kick me three times, getting madder each time. When this does not work, he tries to hit me with his fist. He backs up to to get a running start, but each time I catch his arm and spill him, saying, "I can't let you hurt me." Finally, he speaks.

Hubert: "I'm not coming back to this old school."
Mrs. S: "Oh, don't say that Hubert, because I like you and like having you in our school."

I would not have been understanding his existence situation if I had replied, "You don't want to come back to school?" It might have been better if I had first acknowledged his anger at me.

Hubert was still trying to hurt me. He was continuing to do with words what he could not do with his actions. He thought that he could hurt me by saying he was not coming back to the school. I decided at this point to talk to his need. He needed to know that I like him. I did not want to verify his feeling that the world is a hostile place and that he will have to be clever and cruel to get what he wants, and that I too am part of his hostile world.

Understanding required doing something for this boy. His deepest desire was to live in relationship and I spoke to this need. I moved into an active understanding role. Understanding is active, never passive. There comes a time in understanding when the teacher has to give. I responded in terms of what I felt Hubert was struggling for.

It is not helpful for a child to be able to mistreat adults, especially his parents or his teachers. Psychologically he needs to respect the adults in his life. Mistreating them does not enable him to respect the person in himself, nor does it give him the clue that there is any order or justice in the world. Furthermore, it reinforces a child's false way of solving his problems.

Hubert was filled with hostility and resentment. He was four and a half years old when he started school. He had discovered that if he made a big enough racket, he would get his way. He had also become skilled at irritating other children to make them look bad. He needed to discover in a very existential way that there is a moral structure in the world with which he has to come to terms, and in which he can really live.

A couple of days later Hubert tells me about a dream he had that indicated that he was continuing to work out some of the deeper feelings that contributed to our showdown. Carol and Sam, who appear in the dream, are children in the nursery school.

Hubert: "Mrs. Snyder, I had a dream last night."
Mrs. S: "A dream, Hubert?"
Hubert: "I dreamed that Carol and Sam were having a party in my playroom in our basement and I didn't want them there. So I hit them and made a lot of noise to get them out of there. Then my mother came down and she wouldn't listen to me."
Mrs. S: "You would like to have your mother listen to your troubles, Hubert?"

Hubert: "Yes."

The showdown had a real impact upon Hubert. This dream reveals Hubert's need to exclude his rivals, which is probably derived from his rivalry with his brother. But now he wants to be valued and live in relationship with other people, as the dream about the party indicates. He wants an adult who will help him accomplish this. He is moving toward better integration and is beginning to show internal controls.

Hubert is reaching out for a relationship with me; he also wants the kind of relationship that he feels Sam and Carol have with me. When this relationship comes to him through his feelings, he will begin to be able to care for me. Caring for me will free him to care for others.

Meeting an integrity helps the child with his disorganization. It breaks the circle of hostility that is swirling like a tornado inside the child. It stops the energies that are flowing in the wrong direction. It helps the tension come out so that he is free to come back together again.

Teachers should not depend on showdowns to heal the real source of a child's difficulties. In this case I not only stopped the tornado of hostility; I was able at the same time to offer Hubert relationship. Until one helps a child with the source of his difficulty, he will continue to have eruptions of hostility.

We were trying to heal Hubert so that he would become a fully functioning child with spirit. We did not want him to become blindly submissive.

Here are a couple of incidents that occurred when his younger brother Chester came to school a year later.

> We are outside playing. It was in the fall, and it is not too cold yet. Chester goes to the door and says he wants to go inside because it's too cold.

> Mrs. S: "You want to go in? You don't want to stay out here where it's cold?"
> Chester: (Very demanding) "Yes, I want to play inside."

Mrs. S: "Chester, now it is time to play outside. We finished playing inside today."
(Chester starts kicking the door and stamping his foot.)

Chester: "Open this door right away, I tell you."

Mrs. S: "You want to tell me as hard as you know how that you want to go inside, but this is our time to play outside."

He looks at me in a very puzzled way and walks away.

A week later, at toilet time, Chester goes in first and sits on the toilet a long time, having a bowel movement. This slows up toilet time for the whole group. I keep going back to see if he is done. Finally, I stop to talk with him. We get interested in talking, but he is not getting done on the toilet, so I become silent.

Chester: "I would like to make a mess all over people."
(He closes his fists as if to do it with feces.)

Mrs. S: "Mess up everybody?"

Chester: (Looking at me) "Yes, mess up their faces."

Mrs. S: "You would like to mess me up too?"

Chester: "Yes, mess up your glasses."

Mrs. S: "There is something about me you don't like?"

Chester: "Yes."

Mrs. S: "You don't like it when I make you do things."

Chester: (Looking up at me, startled) "Yes."

Several days later, I go into the bathroom and notice that Chester is playing in the toilet.

Mrs. S: "Chester, when you get through playing in the toilet, wash your hands with soap."

Chester: (In a positive voice) "OK."

I expected that this might happen and hoped I could take it in stride, so that he would not be fixated on this behavior. This was the only time he played in the toilet. Chester made changes fast.

Being a person with integrity may mean having a show-down with a child, as I did when I helped Hubert face his destructive behavior and learn that it would not work. At other times it may mean being present with a child, such as with Chester, in a way that allows him to work things through by himself.

NOT ALLOWING DEVIOUS BEHAVIOR TO SUCCEED

It is important that the child get an honest report of the teacher's feelings. Meeting an integrity means just this. When a child is hurting or misusing someone, he needs an honest report. When adults disguise their feelings they only reinforce devious behavior.

Outside in the play yard, Chester wants one of the big tricycles. But they are being used, so he rides the new smaller black one. As soon as someone leaves a big one, he runs and gets it. Marie gets on the new tricycle that Chester has left and discovers that one of the handles is missing. She rides to me and tells me.

Mrs. S:	"Chester, the handle is gone from the black trike. Where is it?"
	(He doesn't answer.)
Mrs. S:	"Chester, can you tell me where you put the handle from the new trike?"
	(He doesn't answer, so I get down to talk to him.)
Mrs. S:	"Chester, where did you put the handle for the new trike?"
	(His lips move, but no sound comes out.)
Mrs. S:	"You will have to tell me out loud."
	(Again, he just moves his lips.)
Mrs. S:	"Well, Chester, if you can't tell me out loud, you will have to get off this tricycle."
Chester:	"I don't know where it is, Mrs. Snyder, I threw it up there."

Another child who hears this conversation finds the handle and brings it to me.

> Mrs. S: "Chester, if you take off the handle again, you
>   won't be able to ride today. Do you under-
>   stand?"
> Chester: "Yes."

NOT GRANTING SPECIAL PRIVILEGES

Some children believe that if you really care for them, they can have special privileges. This is often true of the youngest child of a family, and it is sometimes true of an only child.

Ryan is the youngest child in his family. It bothers him very much that he cannot do everything as well as his ten-year-old brother and eight-year-old sister. He is used to special treatment at home.

One day during rest period Ryan is moving around bothering the other children.

> Mrs. S: "Ryan, you're bothering the other children."

He stops for a while, then starts again.

> Mrs. S: Ryan, I hope you won't have to rest after every-
>   one else is done."

He keeps moving around.

> Mrs. S: (A while later) "Rest period is over, everybody.
>   But, Ryan, you will have to finish your resting."

Ryan jumps up and takes his mat into the locker room. When I get there he runs into the storage room. I go and get him by the hand and bring him to the locker room.

> Mrs. S: "Ryan, look, I am not going to chase you any-
>   more."
> Ryan: "Let go of my hand. I'm going to kick you."

Mrs. S: "I will not let you go until I am sure you will not try to go into the storage room again."

Ryan: "I'll take you over to my house and put you down the clothes chute."

Mrs. S: "Putting me down your clothes chute would hurt me more than anything you can think of?"

Ryan: "Yes."

(I let go of his hand.)

Mrs. S: "You want to hurt me because you want to do as you please."

Ryan: "That rule is not a good idea about resting after the others are done."

Mrs. S: "You would like for me to let you bother the other children during rest period and not rest afterwards?"

Ryan: "And I'm going in and eat popcorn now."

Mrs. S: "Ryan, you have to do your resting, and if you get it done in time, you will get your popcorn."

Ryan finishes his resting and gets his popcorn.

NOT YIELDING TO RUTHLESS POWER

Neal is a bright, attractive boy who occasionally comes to school thoroughly saturated with the need to tell people off. He will take on the role of his favorite TV character and ruthlessly try to take over the whole school. The children often succumb to his domination because he is so convincing.

In January, Neal's behavior becomes worse. He starts to talk in a rough manner to adults as well as to children. One morning he comes to school and sees a new student teacher.

Neal: "What are you doing here? Get out. I hate you."

The next day in the locker room he finds a stick in one of the lockers and goes after another student teacher, using the stick like a sword.

Neal: "I'm going to cut off your head. Get down on your knees and pray to God."

ST: "It makes you feel strong to talk mean, Neal?" (Neal hesitates, then continues.)

Neal: "Now I have cut off your head anyway. Now you better pray."

On the next day Neal talks to some adults he meets in the hall.

Neal: "Get out of my school. I hate you."

The new student teacher hears this.

ST: "Neal, when you talk like that to people, you make it hard for people to like you."

Neal: "Nobody likes me. I don't care. I hate everybody. And I'm going to throw you through the window."

ST: "That is not a good idea, Neal. You would break the window."

Neal: "I'll throw you out and not break the window."

ST: "That would make you feel good?"

Neal: "Then I'll throw me out."

ST: "You feel very bad?"

Neal: "And I'll kill God, too."

On the next morning Neal arrives in a vile mood. It is obvious that this behavior is becoming part of his identity. Someone needs to break the pattern, and it will have to be a person he cares for and respects. Neal starts to talk roughly to the children on the jungle house. When inner impulses are on the warpath, something very strong is needed.

Neal: "Get out of here. This is for Duncan and me."

Ben is climbing up the slide. Neal pushes him in the face.

Mrs. S: "Neal, you are talking mean to Ben. If you want to play up there, you can't be talking mean."

Neal: "I don't want him up here. Get off."
(He starts pushing again.)

I lift Neal off the jungle house and put him on the floor.

Mrs. S: "You like having Duncan back and you would like to play with him alone. But Neal, when you act like that you can't be up there."
Neal: "I'm going to get back up there. You can't do that to me. Shut up."
(He starts to climb up.)
Mrs. S: "Neal, you are talking mean to me. I don't let children talk that way to me. You will have to sit down until you feel better."

I put him on the window seat and sit down beside him.

Neal: "My mother and dad let me say anything I want to them."
Mrs. S: "I don't believe that Neal. You are too wonderful a boy for them to let you act this way."
Neal: "I can call them liars and they don't care."
Mrs. S: "Then they are not doing a good job of helping you grow up if they let you talk like that. I better talk with them."

This stops his verbal battle. He seems to be thinking. After a while I tell him that he can play. He joins a group of children who are playing house. For the rest of that morning and the following week, he continues to re-establish relationships with me and the other children.

One day that week at toilet time, he looks directly into the face of one of the smaller boys.

Neal: "Glen is really pretty, isn't he?"

This was Neal's true feelings. When he had been acting ruthless and powerful, he could not see others as human beings. They were objects on whom he could vent his hostile self. The showdown helped settle the tornado and released him to feel again.

Dealing with Determined Defiance

A phenomenon of our culture is the child who has never learned to limit himself in any way. He has never experienced any dependable and consistent relationship that helped him learn how to relate responsively.

This kind of child wants everything on his own terms. He cannot differentiate between healthy social requests and cruel demands that deprive him of the right to live his life.

All requests are perceived as a threat to his autonomy and an invasion of his freedom. So he continues to do little irritating things that keep escalating the contest to show that he does not have to come to terms with anybody. He has determined to do as he pleases and no one can stop him. Instead of responding to possibilities of play, he continues the game of testing and teasing to prove that he is more powerful than adults. His actions tell you in no uncertain terms to stay out of his way.

> Joe is a four-year-old boy who had not begun to talk by the time he entered nursery school. There is no physical reason for his silence. He is determined to do as he pleases and has a whole arsenal of weapons to frustrate any adult who gets in his way. After the first time he paints at the easel he starts to put the brushes in the wrong jars. I say to him the same thing I have said to other children with positive results.

> Mrs. S: "Joe, if you put the red brush back into the red jar of paint, it keeps the red bright and clear."

> Joe throws the red brush across the room. Then in rapid succession, he throws the yellow, green, and blue brushes.

> Mrs. S: "Joe, that is not a good idea. We just have to pick them up."

He picks up the jar of red paint and throws it hard. Then he laughs. I quickly put my hand over the remaining jars.

Mrs. S: "Hey, Joe, stop. We just have to clean it up."

At first I clean it up alone. But as Joe begins to feel that I am for him, I can hand him a sponge and he helps me clean up, especially when he sees other children helping me and hears them say, "He is being silly." I tell them that "Joe hasn't learned how to play and have fun yet. He will learn." Gradually, after similar experiences, I can say to him, "Here is the sponge, Joe, clean up the mess." Then he stops making messes.

Usually I try not to get into a head-on battle of wills. But once a child's behavior forces you into this battle, you have to see it through and win so that the child understands that this behavior defeats what he really wants. Allowing a child to control by defiant teasing makes it harder for him to change. It prevents him from learning other modes of being in the world.

If feelings are appropriate, let him express them. But when the child is acting out and trying to control others, he needs to meet an integrity who can terminate his game.

Extreme defiance such as throwing jars of paint, spitting, breaking equipment, and knocking other children down is part of the control game. It is self-destructive and should not be allowed to continue. Only the adult whom the child feels is for him and is offering him an attractive way of life can do anything for that child.

WHAT AN INTEGRITY IS

The children in the episodes in this chapter are children who, at the time, did not feel very good about themselves. They were suffering children. The child who is filled with hostility, the child who needs to be destructive, the defying child, and the child who seeks special privileges, all need healing. At times the necessary healing starts in a head-on encounter with an adult they cannot violate with impunity, who refuses to give in to their controlling maneuvers, with whom they cannot have their way by whining, attacking, or becoming an unbearable nuisance. They need to meet a human dignity who refuses to be reduced to a nonentity or to their own aggressive level of existence, a person who does not allow them to violate other people, or to destroy the justice culture.

Being an integrity that can be encountered does not mean being an impervious, stubborn person always intent on imposing her or his will on all occasions. It does mean being a person in tune with the human in one's self and in all mankind, who cannot easily be pushed out of this relationship. An integrity is a person who affirms a style of living, and not only expresses it, but tunes up and reconstructs her or his behavior in accordance with it. Such people live not by a single value or conclusion, but by a system of values that inform and shape that person's life.

Meeting an integrity is not the same as what is usually thought of as disciplining. Traditional disciplining is more concerned with control and punishment. A teacher or parent who is an integrity is concerned with helping a child learn to handle his angry feelings so that he can be in charge of himself. So the child must feel that he is encountering a significant adult who is for him and will not let him be untrue to himself—one who can understand him and take him into relationship. To be encountered and understood by such a person opens a new chapter in a child's life.

Meeting an integrity not only stops temporarily the undesirable behavior of the child, it starts the child working on his problem. The child's old ways no longer work, and he now has a different world with which to make himself.

I do not mean to imply that this kind of encounter is the only time that the child meets the teacher as an integrity. When the teacher is being understanding, enabling a child to be creative, enjoying relationships, and helping a child face and change aggressive behavior—she is also being an integrity.

Chapter 10

BEING A PRESENCE

Human beings are a relatively new form of life in the long history of the earth. We are more sensitively tuned than any other life, able to live mutually with other persons and delight in them and able to create new futures. Human beings care about their own fate and about what happens to those they love, and are filled with depths of mystery that can never be fully expressed or verbally understood.

When a teacher is present in this fashion in the nursery school, she and the children become "Presences" to each other.

As a Presence, a teacher sees the child as a rich life of feeling, seeing, and intending. She affirms, with everything she is, that it is good that this is so, even though such richness creates problems and conflicts. Perceiving, feeling, and intending, are primary processes of life, and she is for life.

A teacher is a Presence when she holds onto the vision that each child can become a full-functioning person and care for others. Such a teacher keeps saying to herself, "There is a way to reach this child. There is a little self struggling to be free,

208

wanting to live in relationship and wanting to have fun." She keeps out of her mind labels like "problem child," "developmental deviate," "brain-damaged" and other pathological categories, and at the same time she works to free the child from present limitations.

Presence is sensitivity to the possibility trying to express itself in the child at this particular moment. A teacher with such presence is spontaneous enough to let go of images of old behavior when the first glimmer of the new appears. Presence involves responding to the question the child is asking with his current actions, rather than relating to that child on the basis of yesterday's behavior. Growing is continually breaking out in a child even though significant growth sometimes appears in small ways. The child needs to experience the teacher as being a freedom responding to him as a freedom, catching what is being born, and being with it.

Presence involves entering with delight into children's fun and joy, but it is also being an integrity that will not let the child be untrue to himself or the justice culture. Presence involves being available to respond to the needs of an individual child while keeping up with the nursery school's other complexities.

TO A BED WETTER

One morning the children ask me to be the doctor for their dolls. I sit on the window ledge as they bring their sick dolls to me, and I take the dolls and make up different illnesses for them.

Mrs. S:	"Susan must have the measles. Look—she is all broken out. Keep her in bed and give her lots of orange juice."
Jill:	(With laughing eyes) "That isn't measles, Mrs. Snyder. That's jam she got on her at breakfast."
Mrs. S:	"Oh dear, a doctor should know the difference between jam and measles. Maybe a bath would help Susan?"
Jill:	"I guess it's the measles Susan has, and jam too."

To another child's doll, I give a shot for a bad cold. The children always enjoy pretend shots.

In the midst of this play, Hubert brings our big doll and puts her in my lap.

> Hubert: "Mrs. Snyder, you have to do something for this baby. She wets her bed every night, and I can't make her stop. You just have to do something to make her stop wetting her bed."
>
> Mrs. S: "Your dolly must feel very bad about wetting the bed. She wants not to wet the bed very much. All children wet their beds at first, and then after awhile they don't wet their beds anymore. You must be very kind to her. I think it would help your dolly if you would rock her for a while."

As Hubert takes his doll tenderly, his whole feeling tone changes. He is nearly five years old, the oldest boy in the school, and wetting the bed at night is his problem.

WHEN A CHILD IS AFRAID

Being a Presence is sensing the fears of children and trying to help them work through the fears.

One day at juice time Jill says to me.

> Jill: "You know, I sleep with my eyes open at night."
>
> Mrs. S: "You sleep with your eyes open, Jill?"

All the children start talking about sleeping with their eyes open.

> Jill: "I sleep with mine open because I'm afraid."
>
> Mrs. S: "Afraid of the dark?"

This starts another wave of conversation. As a teacher, I know that the best way to help a child get over her fears is to keep her talking about them.

Jane:	"I keep my door open at night."
Carol:	"I keep my light on at night."
Dick:	"I have a night light on my floor."
Ron:	"I have a light with a sheep on it."
Mrs. S:	"It seems different at night when you can't see?"
Abe:	"I'm afraid of the thunder and lightning."
	(Abe's bed is on the third floor under a slanting roof.)
Mrs. S:	"It's noisy and scary, Abe?"
Abe:	"Yes, and you can't not hear it."

I keep them talking until it seems that they have finished.

After each bad storm the children talk about it again. I tell them that storms are something you can't control, but that you can learn to do what is safe. Upsetting events announced on radio and TV also have to be talked through. To a fearful child, anything strange calls up his fears. This kind of child needs additional help in building ego strength and discovering whom he can trust.

IN DESPAIR

Being a Presence is seeing the depths of despair that come to a child whose world has gone to pieces and to whom all strangers are a disintegrating experience. Being a Presence means verbalizing a girl's feelings so that she can put some structure to the jungle inside her.

One morning Carol comes skipping into the room. It is good to see her skipping because she has come a long way to get the freedom to do so. But when she sees a strange man in the room, she freezes. Her face goes blank.

When her mother comes to her, Carol clings to her. Her mother tries to make up a game by telling Carol that she will go out and that Carol should open the door and let her in. But nothing works, so her mother walks her to the coat room. When

I get there Carol is sitting in her locker, all hunched up with her arms over her face. I get down to talk to her.

Mrs. S: "Carol, you don't like having a strange man in our school?"

Carol: "No. Tell him to go away."

Mrs. S: "There is something about him you don't like?"

Carol: "Yes."

Mrs. S: "He reminds you of someone you don't like?"

Carol: "Yes. Tell him to go away."

Mrs. S: "He has gone, Carol. Usually we don't have strange people in our school, but he's a teacher and he wanted to talk to me about his boys and girls."

Carol: "Oh."

Carol walks slowly into the school. Later that morning she is painting a picture at the easel. She is working very hard on it, using big strokes and lots of paint.

Mrs. S: "This is an interesting picture you have painted, Carol."

Carol: "See, it's a jungle. See, a jungle, and it goes round and round and you can't get out."
(She uses her arm to follow the lines of her painting.)

Mrs. S: "There doesn't seem to be any way out?"

Carol: "No."

Carol continued to work through her confusion. She came back to the nursery school for a second year, and by the end of that time she was a full-functioning child ready for kindergarten.

To A Child Who May Have To Live With A Physical Handicap

Being a Presence means helping a girl who may have to live with a physical handicap.

Sally is a wonderful, happy child. She wears traction straps on her legs to correct them. Unless you knew they were under her pants, you would not believe they were there. No one thinks about them. She climbs and runs better than many boys. The morning is never long enough for her to finish all the playing she wants to do.

One morning in December, her father tells me that the doctor wants Sally to have some tests to determine whether she has a physical handicap. The day after the tests, while the family is still awaiting the results, Sally arrives early at school. She is her usual happy self and is anxious to start playing. I have to go to the office across the street, so I take her with me. The street is icy, so on the way back I pick her up to carry her across the street.

Sally:	"They did the tests yesterday."
Mrs. S:	"At the doctor's?"
Sally:	"Why did it have to happen to me?"
Mrs. S:	"You can't figure out why it should happen to you?"
Sally:	"But why did it happen to me? With all the other children? Why?"
Mrs. S:	"To you. This is the hard part."
Sally:	"But my daddy says I'll be all right."
Mrs. S:	"You would like to believe this?"
Sally:	"Yes."
Mrs. S:	"I believe it, Sally. I believe you will be all right."

I put her down and she runs into the room to play. Earlier in the school year she had called me on our play telephone in the nursery school.

Sally:	"Mrs. Snyder, the telephone is ringing."
	(I put one hand to my ear and start talking through the other hand.)
Mrs. S:	"Hello, is this you, Sally?"
Sally:	"Doctor, you must come and see Susan [a doll]. She won't keep on her twisters [traction straps]. She keeps taking them off."
Mrs. S:	"Susan is having trouble with her twisters?"

Sally:	"Yes, she won't leave them on. She keeps taking them off. She keeps them on all day until two o'clock. Then she won't leave them on any longer."
Mrs. S:	"She gets along until two o'clock, then she has to take them off?"
Sally:	"Yes. You better come over and help her."
Mrs. S:	"Well, do you suppose it will help her if she knows that she will not have to wear them all of her life? That she only has to wear them a little longer?"
Sally:	"Yes, I'll tell her."
Mrs. S:	"All right. Good-bye."
Sally:	"But there is something else. She likes Dr. X, but not Dr. Z."
Mrs. S:	"She needs to see two doctors?"
Sally:	"Yes, Dr. X is very nice."
Mrs. S:	"She feels good about him."
Sally:	"Yes, but she doesn't like Dr. Z."
Mrs. S:	"She needs to see Dr. Z to help her, but he doesn't seem so kind?"
Sally:	"Yes. And there's something else."
Mrs. S:	"Something more?"
Sally:	"Yes. Susan just doesn't like to take a bath!"
Mrs. S:	"Susan doesn't like a bath?"
Sally:	"She doesn't like the soap. It hurts her legs."
Mrs. S:	"The soap hurts her. Perhaps there would be a kind of soap . . ."
Sally:	"Good-bye."

Sally had wonderful parents who did a good job explaining things to her. At school she was just trying to work things out so that she could be sure. Fortunately, the results showed that Sally did not have a permanent physical handicap.

ENJOYING WHAT IS HAPPENING

Sometimes a teacher is being a Presence when she just enjoys what a child is saying.

> Sam: "What, Mrs. Snyder?"

At first I answer matter-of-factly.

> Mrs. S: "What do you mean, Sam?"

Then I see his dancing eyes.

> Sam: "What, Mrs. Snyder?"

This time I realize that he just wants to relate in fun. Sam is very interested in words.

> Mrs. S: "What white wiffin woofer went woo woo?"

This is pure delight to him and he follows me across the room with laughing eyes.

> Sam: "Say that again, Mrs. Snyder."

This exchange illustrates the simple delight of being yourself with a feeling of fun. It is also responding relevantly to his excitement.

DELIGHT TOGETHER

The children enjoy playing on top of the ventilator in our school yard after they know what it is. On the first day of school, May seems fearful when she looks down into the ventilator.

> Mrs. S: "May, that's the ventilator where fresh air is taken in for the building."
> (I step on top.)
> "See, the air comes in the top and goes through that screen, then into the building so there is good fresh air inside."
> (She looks down and notices there were two small cars down inside.)

May: "Get the cars out."
Dale: (Who had been in the school last year) "That's Michael's blue car down there."
May: "Get them out."
Dale: "You can't get them out."
Mrs. S: "That's right, Dale. The top is too heavy to take off. It is so strong we can step on it."
          (Dale gets on with me and points down.)
Dale: "That's our pretend zoo."
Mrs. S: "There is the giraffe down there. I'll bet he is hungry. I will have to find something for him to eat."
          (I pick up a leaf and put it down. Dale gets some weeds.)
Dale: "Here, tiger. Nice tiger. Grrr."
Mrs. S: "That fierce tiger was glad to get something to eat."
          (Dale smiles and feels strong, then he goes for more food.)
May: "This is for the elephant. He has a long nose."
Harold: "This is for the alligator with sharp teeth."
Mrs. S: "You have to be careful when you feed alligators with sharp teeth so that they don't bite your hand."
Harold: "You feed him, Mrs. Snyder."
Mrs. S: "If you hold it like this, I think you can do it so he doesn't bite your hand."
          (He carefully "feeds" the alligator.)

It wasn't long before most of the children in the school joined in the fun with our pretend zoo. They added a kangaroo, gorilla, dinosaur, lion, spider, cats, dogs, pigs, frogs, and chickens, making the appropriate noise for each animal. It was a noisy zoo.

A ventilator that had seemed strange and somewhat threatening to the children became something that could be stepped on, and something that offered all kinds of play possibilities. A group became Presences to each other by the spinning of our imaginations, and it was the beginning of all kinds of imaginary play during the year. Sometimes the ventilator became an airplane, a boat, a jail, or a place to dance on, and when it snowed it became a good warming house. But the best thing it became was the zoo with its hungry animals.

Children Being A Presence to Teachers

Children who live in a caring atmosphere take on this caring for each other and for their teachers.

At the beginning of the spring quarter, Tom, a new student teacher, comes into the school for the first time. He had never had any experience with young children. Four-year-old Estelle notices him sitting in a corner of the school yard looking very serious. Estelle goes to him, touches his shoulders, and comes close to his face.

Estelle:	"Haven't you had any birthdays?"
Tom:	"Yes, I've had birthdays."
	(Feeling awkward about it.)
Estelle:	"Didn't your mother bake you cakes?"
Tom:	"Yes, my mother baked me cakes."
Estelle:	"And didn't she put candles on them?"
Tom:	"Yes, I had candles on my cakes."
Estelle:	"Then why are you so sad?"

Tom was both upset and greatly touched by such kind concern coming from a little girl. It helped him relax. He even smiled and felt at ease. Children became real people to him.

Fulfillment for Teacher and Child

Presence is an important word for the teacher to keep in her mind. It sums up all that we have been talking about. It tells us what an *I* is, and what we hope to meet in children. With the help of this word, we can recover our identity as an adult who is good to be around children. *Presence* tells us what the child loses when we fail to relate as a Presence.

Presence says to a child:

> "I am here—right in this situation. I am not paying attention to somebody else, or talking without listening.

> "I'm for you, I'm with you. I'm on the side of your growth— permanently. To me you are not a problem or a discipline case, nor clay to be shaped by me; but a momentum to exist. You are a power and have a right to be. I feel in you the pulse of life.

> I accept you as a fellow human being whom I believe in. No matter how we may disagree, we believe in something together. No matter how hard we struggle, I will not reject you. We will always get back together, I too am something you must take account of. Every so often, I am lost in wonder, amazement, and delight when I meet you.

Presence is a fascinating mystery that is in motion, becoming more than it was a moment ago. What was defeat, a mistake, a problem, is being changed into thought, new relationship, new attempt. Such Presence enlarges the meaningful space in which a child moves. Creation is going on.

The teacher who holds onto a definition of herself as a Presence, who keeps growing in her ability to understand the existence of a child, and who is an integrity that can be encountered, is significantly person.

A SYNOPSIS OF SIX BASIC CONCEPTS

This synopsis is a cognitive map that explains the specific meaning and structure of the most essential words and phrases used in the book. An effort is made to identify the important components of each concept and some of the sources that have contributed to its development. Taken together, these interrelated concepts form a cluster of ideas that describe a style of being human and a view point from which we live with children.

JUSTICE CULTURE

A Justice Culture is a system of love for everybody in a learning and fun environment. The primary goal is to produce full-functioning children who can operate with vitality out of inner feelings and meanings, and care deeply for others.

(1)

A Justice Culture is a creative fidelity to each other's growth. A person knows that others will stand up, not only for their own rights, but for justice for others and to the whole. "When one is hurt, all are hurt." The joy of one lights up others.

The approach to others is constructive and redemptive, not punitive, derogative, or coercive. Control and obedience are not ends in themselves.

(2)

In a Justice Culture all are in the covenant of first class citizens. Teachers enable children to function and be in relationship. They are participants and examples, not centers of arbitrary power who are above the law.

Justice is an essential on-going process. There are established ways of living together and working through conflicts. Feelings are understood and constructively processed within a structure of honesty and fairness. Natural consequences are experienced. Children are not hit, teased, threatened, or terrorized. Justice is never understood as requiring punishment or sanctioning revenge. Those who misbehave or withdraw are healed and restored to healthy functioning.

(3)

A Justice Culture is a corporateness. All share in its creation. Responsibility is felt to keep it going. Many Life Worlds are in healthy relationship and each is better able to function as a person.

This corporate group has an identity, a territory, and a distinctive style that cannot be violated or profaned with impunity. Members will resist invasion of its life space and destruction of its ethic.

A Justice Culture is a little community of people, trying to bring itself off in a precarious and sometimes tragic world. Justice is basic to their identity. It is the essential process and intention that structures and shapes their culture.

A Justice Culture is the opposite of anarchy or an individualism where people are always looking out for "number one" and "doing their own thing." It is the opposite of terrorism where each does to others what he pleases and power needs no justification. It is the opposite of authoritarianism where the power of a few is used to force others into obedience and unquestioning conformity.

(4)

A Justice Culture is a culture of meanings. Each person's behavior is understood in the light of their own meanings and Life World. Change and growth are enabled by the interiorization and formation of meanings, not by mechanically rewarding and punishing responses. As people begin to operate out of a fullness of personal meanings the need for external direction and control diminishes.

A Justice Culture is guided by what is known to be the meaning of the "Highest and Best." Basic standards of excellence and rightness are recognized which are above individual whims and tastes. There is a transcendence over what happens to which all can appeal and by which power is governed. Life-giving structures challenge us and make self-correction possible.

Culture is the meanings which generations of people have wrested out of life, and those they are now manufacturing. Corporateness is not merely a social organization but a society made possible by shared meanings and interpretations. The culturing of meanings is always going on. Each member must have access to the process, be understood and taken account of. Shared experiences and their mutually arrived at interpretations become "significant symbols" that organize life and call forth creative energies.

CONSCIENCE

Conscience is deeply caring for self and others, and the competencies and meanings that empower this caring.

(1)

Conscience is-

–the thrust to become a significant and full-functioning person. The push toward incarnation. To *be* a truth, rather than merely to know or talk about it.

–the hunger to be in relationship. That which moves us to reconcile with those whom we have alienated or let down.

–the continuing search for rightness with the "Highest and Best," combined with a fidelity to what we believe in.

–the move to transcend what is, and what we have been. We are dissatisfied with shortcomings and mediocrities. We are not neutral in respect to justice and injustice, honesty and phoniness, truth and monstrous lies.

(2)

Conscience is "the call of possibility." (Heidegger) Also the "yes" we give to a chance to enable something better become real.

With conscience, all dimensions of time (future-past-present) can *be* in a new way. We fashion a preferred style of Life World.

(3)

Much of conscience is the significant adults and respected companions whom we have interiorized. Conscience is largely learned by "modeling" and participation.

(4)

Conscience is an internal governance system. Understandings of self and the outside world are integrated into a self-in-world. An essential centered self is maintained.

Conscience always works with an image of what kind of world this is. It sizes up who is to be dealt with. Within a person's conscience is a somewhat enduring frame of orientation which determines perceptions, interpersonal strategies, and world building. It awakens or deadens the energies of joyous self-giving.

(5)

Conscience power comes from the experiences of being cared for, the sensing of other persons as struggling, suffering, exulting selves trying for Life World, and the development of interpersonal competencies.

(6)

Healthy conscience requires competencies in understanding, processing and communicating feelings, and constructive activity with others.

(7)

Conscience is integrity work. Trueing-up the self, choosing between better and worse, moving toward dependable identity, resisting invasion and disintegration.

Going for wholeness rather than remaining fragmented and unstoried. Being genuine rather than inauthentic.

****

With healthy conscience, we exist as a center of love and freedom, within warm membership in a group of respected compatriots.

SOCIALITY

We believe in each other and in something together. We can count on each other.

(1)

In a true community of life something of each of us dwells in the other. We have interiorized, in a respecting way, the self-in-world that others are. Our own Life World is created, in part, from these interiorizations. We interiorize into the deepest regions of the self the valuings of ourselves by significant adults as well as their manner of relating to others.

Interiorizing is a concept derived from George Herbert Mead. It is not the same as copying behavior or internalizing something—which can be done without integrating it within the central self. Without this process of interiorizing there is no intersubjectivity. (Merleau-Ponty)

(2)

Some of the words and phrases the group uses are understood in about the same way by all. They dependably call forth congruent action and we all know that they will. They come out of common, and sometimes intense, experiences. Some become "significant symbols" that organize our meanings and call forth our energies. (Mead)

***

We are not alone. We can give and receive communication since we share each other's memories and pictures in our minds. We can get things done and grow.

LIFE WORLD

A child goes forth . . . and the persons, things, pulsings of earth life become part of this child for that day and for all days. He interiorizes and symbolizes them. He reorganizes them into the project of his being-in-the-world.

(1)

The human mind is intentionality. It forms gestalts, the most basic being the Life World. Bits and pieces of "earth" and ourselves are put into a workable pattern. The self is a worlding process.

A Life World is *lived*. It is not just an intellectual world view to which the self is uncommitted.

(2)

A Lived Life World is formed out of the interaction of our energies and the energies of our environment.

A Preferred Life World, that has a rightness to it, also exists as a picture in our mind. We try to bring it off. It we cannot, we feel we have been denied being. This Life World has become our life story and identity. When the stable organization of a meaningful Life World comes apart, we, too, become disintegrated.

(3)

Always, to some degree, the lived and preferred Life Worlds are a joint creation of ourselves and the outside world. The world around us is also forming energies! (It is a bit hard on us to learn this.)

(4)

A Life World is an accessible network of significant memories and symbols with which to recognize, interpret, and invent moments of worlding. Unless we understand the worlding going on in a child's mind, at best we are clumsy.

(5)

A Life World is unique to that person and a variation of the corporate Life World contemporaries are creating. Worlding takes place in the midst of Life Worlds.

(6)

To be human is to have a project. For the moment everything has meaning within that project. (A tricycle is not an object but is part of a project in an arena of action on its way of becoming meaningful Life World for the child.)

(7)

A person is strategies for bringing off a preferred Life World . . . a world fit for hiding and flight . . . or a world for fighting and looking out for "number one" . . . or fit for pleasuring . . . or a world fit for creating together . . .

***

As teachers we are developing Life Worlds and competencies in worlding.

BEING

Being is spirited existence. "I am. I am able. I am a member." "The world is an exciting place. It's fun to be with people. Thinking together makes it more fun."

(1)

Being means being person; a caring, struggling, feeling, interpreting, inventing, participating, and worlding self. A self that is becoming something in particular, that lives knowing what to be true to. In touch with self and the being of other people.

(2)

Being is unique.

"And there is nobody else in the whole world exactly like you." "I am for your growth as a person."

The species "humankind" becomes incarnate.

(3)

The language of being is active and participatory, not frozen or possessive.

Being rather than *having*. "Being something" rather than "having something," "being in relationship" rather than "having relationship", "being integrity" rather than "having integrity", as if integrity was a package you carry around and occasionally exhibit, a trait rather than a state of existence.

Being is "living form." Not just a structure, but a *forming* form that creates many structures and events.

(4)

Being is a duration of time. (Bergson) "Up bubbles the stream of time," bringing up to date the heritage of the past. The self projects futures, venturing beyond already established satisfactions.

***

"Only he knows the truth who participates in the truth".

(Kierkegaard)

PRESENCE

Unmistakably here. Through the rush and things of the world, a voice and a face from the realm of the personal . . . appears. A "Thou" is here to be taken account of.

(1)

Fully here. Not meandering around, playing games with others, at war with itself. An integrity.

(2)

A Holy – not to be violated, profaned, ignored, treated as a thing – is developing its true nature in my presence. I do not control it. Nor would I want to.

(3)

A bearer of destiny is present. Help is here, able to set in motion a transformation of the situation. There is an invitation to create together.

(4)

A Depth . . . a facinating moreness yet to become unhidden. . . . is addressing me-in-particular, in my uniqueness at this moment. The relationship is starkly I-Thou.

****

"The world comes to me in the form of a person" (Martin Buber)

BIBLIOGRAPHY

This is a highly selective bibliography, giving sources of seed thoughts rather than a complete list of references.

PULSE OF LIFE

Dewey, J. *Experience and education.* New York: MacMillan, 1938. Theory of Experience, pp. 12–22; Social Control, pp. 53–68.

Eiseley, L. *The immense journey.* New York: Vintage Books, Random House, 1957.

Henri, R. *The art spirit.* New York: Lippincott, 1923. The Hour of Expression, pp. 105, 145, 123, 233; "My People," pp. 189–90, 240–245.

Merleau-Ponty, M. *The primacy of perception.* J. Edie (Ed.). Evanston: Northwestern University Press, 1964, pp. 12–27.

HOW HEALTHY CONSCIENCE DEVELOPS

Barrett, W. *The illusion of technique.* New York: Anchor/Doubleday, 1978. A critique of current thought in the modern era, and a statement of his position. The line of argument in the whole book is important. Essential positions are stated on pp. 104–105, 173–176, 222–225, 234, 248–251, 294, 313–314, 345, and xviii–xx.

Heidegger, M. *Being and time.* New York: Harper, 1962. Being as Care, pp. 235–244; Authentic-Potentiality-for-Being. Conscience, pp. 312–322, 370–374, 385–388.

Vygotskii, L. S. *Thought and language.* E. Haufmann & G. Vakar (Ed. and Trans.). Cambridge: M.I.T. Press, 1962. Inner Speech, pp. 130–153.

A Child is a Life World

Adler, A. *What life should mean to you.* Boston: Little, Brown, 1931. Meaning of Life, pp. 2–24.

Erikson, E. H. *Identity and the life cycle.* New York: International University Press, 1959. Growth and Crises of Healthy Personality, pp. 50–100.

King, M. *Heidegger's philosophy.* New York: Macmillan Company, 1964. The Being of Man, pp. 46–57; The Worldishness of World, pp. 70–85.

Lawrence, N. M. *Readings in existential phenomenology.* N. Lawrence & D. O'Connor (Eds.). Englewood Cliffs, New Jersey: Prentice Hall, 1967. Lived Space: O. F. Bollnow, pp. 178–186; Spontaneity: Eugene Minkowski, pp. 168–177.

May, R. *Existence.* R. May, E. Angel, & H. F. Ellenberger (Eds.). New York: Basic Books, 1958. Origins, pp. 10–12; Contribution of Existential Psychotherapy, pp. 37–45, 55–91; The Existential Analysis School of Thought, pp. 200–213.

Tagiuri, R. & Petrullo, L. *Person perception and interpersonal behavior.* Palo Alto: Stanford University Press, 1958. Person Perception: Fritz Heider, pp. 22–31.

Breaking Out of Limitations

Henry, J. *Culture against man.* New Jersey: Random House, 1963. Pathways to Madness, pp. 322–388.

Jackson, D. (Ed.). *Etiology of schizophrenia.* New York: Basic Books, 1960. Family Dynamics, pp. 323–387.

Enabling Through the Understanding Mode of Conversation

Duncan, H. *Communication and the social order.* Communication and the Emergence of Self, New York, Bedminster Press, 1962 pp. 73–80; Consummatory Experiences, pp. 82–91.

Heidegger, M. *Being and time.* New York: Harper, 1962. Understanding, pp. 184–187, 346–347, 385–388.

Miller, D. L. *George Herbert Mead:* Self, language and world. Austin: University of Texas, 1973. The Fundamental Concept of Sociality.

Roger, C. *Client-centered therapy.* Boston: Houghton Mifflin, 1951.

Roger, C. *Freedom to learn.* Columbus, Ohio: Charles E. Merrill, 1969. Being in Relationship, pp. 221–237.

Strauss, A. L. (Ed.). *Social psychology of George Herbert Mead.* Chicago: Chicago University Press, 1964. Self, pp. 212–246.

INTEGRITY THAT CAN BE ENCOUNTERED

Colm, H. *The existential approach to psychotherapy with adults and children.* New York and London: Grune & Stratton, 1966. Healing As Participation, pp. 151–156; Play As Communication, pp. 20–21.

Merleau-Ponty, M. *Phenomenology of perception.* C. Smith (Trans.). New York: Humanities Press, 1962. Other People and the Human World, pp. 346–365.

Merleau-Ponty, M. *The primacy of perception.* J. Edie (Ed.). Evanston: Northwestern University Press, 1964. Child's Relation With Others, pp. 96–155.

BEING A PRESENCE

Buber, M. *Between man and man.* R. G. Smith (Trans.). London: K. Paul, 1947. Dialogue, pp. 1–39; Education, pp. 83–103.

Buber, M. *I-thou* R. G. Smith (Trans.). Edinburg: T&T Clark, 1937.

Heidegger, M. *Being and time.* New York: Harper and Brothers, 1962. Discourse, pp. 55–56. 207–221.

Marcel, G. *The mystery of being.* London: Harvill Press, 1950. Presence as a Mystery, pp. 204–208.

Marcel, G. *Homo viator.* E. Crawfurd (Trans.). New York: Harper, Torchbook, 1962. Creative Fidelity, pp. 90–97, 116–124.

Snyder, R. *On Becoming Human.* Nashville and New York, 1967. Abingdon Press.

INDEX OF EPISODES

This index is designed to facilitate the use of the episodes in this book for in-service training, parent education, presentations, and discussions among teachers, parents, staff, or students. These episodes can be shared in their entirety, or used statement by statement; reading the child's statement and constructing one's own response or action before comparing it with what the teacher actually said or did. Episodes that particularly lend themselves to this approach are marked with an asterisk (*) in the index.

234

INDEX